A Company of Businessmen

The Hudson's Bay Company and Long-Distance Trade, 1670-1730

Elizabeth Mancke

Rupert's Land Research Centre
1988

University of Winnipeg
Winnipeg, Canada

Manke, Elizabeth, 1954—
    A Company of Businessmen: The Hudson's Bay
    Company and Long-Distance Trade,
    1670-1730

© 1988 by the Rupert's Land Research Centre
Printed in Canada
ISBN 0-921206-04-6

A Company of Businessmen

A Company of Businessmen

Rupert's Land Research Centre
University of Winnipeg
515 Portage Avenue
Winnipeg, Canada
R3B 2E9

Timothy F. Ball
Director

Jennifer S.H. Brown
General Editor

CONTENTS

LIST OF TABLES

FOREWORD

In 1960 E. E. Rich wrote that in the seventeenth and eighteenth centuries the Hudson's Bay Company deliberately developed a number of key trading practices to accommodate Indian exchange traditions.[1] The economist Abraham Rotstein recast Rich's thesis in the theoretical framework of Karl Polanyi.[2] In support of his notion that the fur trade was a kind of treaty trade Rotstein cited the existence of gift exchanges and rigid official price schedules as central aspects of the business. In this type of exchange political considerations, mostly those of the natives, rather than market forces were presumed to be the key determinants in setting exchange rates. Donald Freeman and I challenged this, suggesting that the prices which prevailed at trading posts in the 18th century reflected local market circumstances.[3] Contrary to Rich's and Rotstein's assertions, we argued that Indians were sensitive to prices; we presented trading post data as one line of evidence in support of our position.

The controversy about the nature of Indian economic behavior in the early fur trade continues to the present. Those who are predisposed to accept or reject the Indians as economic men line up on one or the other side of the debate. So long as the focus remains centered on the Indian participants any further insights into the eighteenth century fur trade are unlikely.

It is for this reason that Elizabeth Mancke's monograph is refreshing and important. She has approached the subject from a different perspective. She directs our attention toward the problems the English managers faced in conducting long-distance trade. Native exchange practices were only one aspect of the issue. More fundamental was the problem of creating some semblance of stability in the face of never-ending uncertainty. For

---

[1] E. E. Rich, "Trade Habits and Economic Motivations among the Indians of North America," in _Canadian Journal of Economics and Political Science_ 26 (1960): 35-53.

[2] A. Rotstein, "Fur Trade and Empire: An Institutional Analysis," Ph.D. dissertation, University of Toronto, 1967.

[3] Arthur J. Ray and Donald B. Freeman, _Give Us Good Measure_ (Toronto: University of Toronto Press, 1978).

guidance, the London directors drew on European traditions and the experiences of merchants who were active in other trading spheres. In this way they tailored a system that was well-suited to the particular circumstances of both the Canadian subarctic and London.

In this study Mancke concentrates on administration and management. Her findings have significance that goes well beyond the debate about Indian trading habits. They suggest that the Hudson's Bay Company's persistence as a trading organization has to be seen in terms of business management successes. This casts doubt on Harold Innis' assertion that the eventual English dominance over the French was due to their achievement of technological superiority. Mancke's findings also lead us to reconsider another shibboleth of Canadian history -- that the Hudson's Bay Company was conservative and reactive from the beginning and therefore rarely ever able to hold its own against contemporary opponents. If this trading company was so inflexible, why was it the only one to survive through the mercantile and industrial eras? Striking to me is the fact that the business systems that the Hudson's Bay Company developed during the formative years were so well-suited to the enterprise that many of the management and accounting elements remained in place until the late nineteenth century. In other words, company "conservatism" may have been rooted in the highly successful management responses made in the formative years; thereafter, only fine tuning was required to keep the company viable. Company commissioner C. C. Chipman (1891-1910) said the company's earlier history showed it to be a "progressive conservative" organization. Mancke's study gives us good reason to consider this proposition.

Arthur J. Ray
Vancouver

ACKNOWLEDGEMENTS

This study began as a research paper for Arthur J. Ray at the University of British Columbia. He has been generous in sharing his expertise as well as supporting me in the academic community. A summer research fellowship from the University of British Columbia funded my trip to the Hudson's Bay Company Archives in the Provincial Archives of Manitoba. Shirlee A. Smith and the staff at the archives provided first-rate professional advice and assistance. Keith Ralston proved a thoughtful and critical colleague that summer. Earlier drafts of this manuscript were typed by Lori Thompson under heroic conditions. Jennifer Brown, general editor of the Rupert's Land Research Centre, edited the manuscript for publication with care and thoughtfulness. She and Wilson Brown provided hospitality and companionship in generous measure while I was in Winnipeg to finish the publication preparations. Wilson Brown, Hugh Grant, Ann Harper-Fender, John McCusker, Peter Moogk, Richard Unger, and William Wray read and commented on the manuscript. At the University of Winnipeg, Linda Gladstone aided in the final preparation of the manuscript and Renée Jones helped compile the index. The Rupert's Land Historical Studies Fund made publication possible.

For all of this support, advice, help, and collegiality I am deeply grateful. As with many endeavors, the first word of thanks is also the last. Arthur J. Ray gave me enough support that if I failed the fault was mine alone and enough independence to fashion the final results as I saw fit. For the results I am alone responsible.

x

INTRODUCTION

This examination of the Hudson's Bay Company management from 1670 to 1730 focuses on the company's place in the history of the expansion of Europe, and more particularly, on the management of long-distance trade as one aspect of that expansion. Central to this analysis are the objectives of the company, the way it maximized opportunities and minimized risk and uncertainty, the organization of its affairs to coordinate the barter trade in North America and the London fur market, and their influence on the long-term survival of the company.

An attempt to convert the beaver value, by which the Indian paid for European trade goods, to a sterling value first prompted this study. Since the Hudson's Bay Company's North American rate of exchange of furs for trade goods fluctuated very little between 1670 and 1870, the years when that rate was established were the logical point to begin the inquiry. The clues to solving this problem directed me through a maze involving the compilation, correlation, and analysis of trade good prices and fur prices in London. This peregrination led to the solution of the initial question, but also revealed the difficulty of drawing a simple correlation between the price of trade goods, the price of furs, and the financial stability of the company. During its first sixty years, 1670 to 1730, trade good prices fluctuated little and beaver prices dropped precipitously before stabilizing. Yet despite the narrowed gap in trade good prices and fur prices the company, after nearly fifty years in business, began to distribute annual dividends. Dropping beaver prices parallelled the price declines of other colonial commodities, caused by rapid increases in supply and the ease of substitution afforded by the relatively homogeneous character of most colonial goods. How the company survived this transition wrought by the growth in the North American fur trade became the focus of this study, and price movements a trail to be followed in tracing long-term trends in the company's fortunes.

One of the enduring myths of Western civilization is that of the trader venturing away from hearth and home, risking life and limb, and returning to fame and fortune. The adventures of Marco Polo excite the homebound

1

imagination of succeeding generations.   Every school
child knows that Christopher Columbus landed on the
shores of the western hemisphere while searching for a
route to the riches of the Orient.   Conquistadors and fur
traders pushed into the interiors of the American
continents searching for gold, silver, and furs.

The ease with which we discount this folk mythology
for its extravagant embroidering of reality does not
wholly emasculate it.   Thus, in more tempered scholarly
accounts historians and economists have often concluded
that long-distance trade, almost by its very nature,
generated greater profits than did domestic enterprises.
Contemporary scholarship reveals an ongoing, lively, and
at times heated debate on the relationship between long-
distance trade and profits, long-distance trade and
industrial growth, and long-distance trade and the present economic hegemony of the industrialized nations.
Scholars such as Immanuel Wallerstein argue that the
present economic disparity between regions of the world
has its origins in the fifteenth century, a watershed
between precapitalistic and capitalistic business practices.   Integral to this argument is the importance of
European expansion beyond the Mediterranean and Baltic
commercial arenas of the medieval world. Merchant capitalism, whose salient features were buying cheap and
selling dear, high profits, and the exploitation of
labor, propelled European economic development.   The profits gained from trade, and especially colonial trades,
fuelled European economic growth and made possible the
Industrial Revolution.   European long-distance trade
transferred large amounts of wealth from the periphery
(the underdeveloped areas of the world) to the core
states (northern Europe and later the United States).
Had this not happened, it is suggested, the core states
could not have experienced such rapid growth vis-a-vis
the periphery.[4]

Historians challenging this theory argue that the
levels of profit in colonial trades such as tobacco,
slaves, and sugar were not as high as has long been
presumed, and were often not as high as the profits made
in domestic commerce and industry. Drawing on studies of
the profitability of colonial trades, Patrick O'Brien
suggests that trade with the periphery was not large
enough to substantiate the claim that it was a primary

---

[4]Immanuel Wallerstein, The Modern World System (New
York: Academic Press, 1974).

source of capital for the Industrial Revolution.[5] Richard Grassby in a study of the formation of seventeenthcentury business fortunes and merchant capitalism challenges the belief that overseas trade created many, if not most of the great English fortunes. Trade provided advancement for men of small fortunes; financial services and the manipulation of money made the large fortunes.[6]

As evidence accumulates which undermines the thesis that high profits from long-distance trade precipitated the world's present economic disparity, it nonetheless remains difficult, and premature, to cast aside the notion that trade, as a nexus between Europe and the rest of the world, holds a clue to understanding the world's economic development. The historical emphasis given to overseas expansion has indeed exaggerated its place in the European economy and overshadowed less spectacular enterprises.[7] Nevertheless, the changes which resulted from the expansion of Europe recommend the merits of studying its dynamic in detail, even if we fail to discover the inflated profits which it seemed to promise. Cross-cultural contact, changes in labor structures, and the extension of European political control to Asia, Africa, and the Americas all found expression in transoceanic trade. These processes increasingly attract the attention of scholars in their attempt to understand the integration of the world and the growth of Western economic hegemony in the last five centuries.[8]

---

[5]Patrick O'Brien, "European Economic Development: the Contribution of the Periphery," Economic History Review, 2d ser. 35 (1982): 1-18; Immanuel Wallerstein, "European Economic Development: A Comment on O'Brien," EHR, 2d ser. 36 (1983): 580-83; and O'Brien, "European Economic Development: A Reply," ibid., 584-85.

[6]R. Grassby, "English Merchant Capitalism in the Late Seventeenth Century: the Composition of Business Fortunes," Past and Present 46 (1970): 103.

[7]Kristof Glamann, "The Changing Patterns of Trade," in The Economic Organization of Early Modern Europe, vol. 5, Cambridge Economic History of Europe, eds. E. E. Rich and C. H. Wilson (Cambridge: Cambridge University Press, 1977), pp. 191-93.

[8] Two recent attempts at broad synthetic models of the importance of trade are Eric Wolf, Europe and the People Without History (Berkeley: University of California Press, 1982); and Philip D. Curtin, Cross-cultural Trade in World History, (Cambridge University Press, 1984).

The historic importance of long-distance trade to the growth of the British economy, Jacob Price argues, may have been qualitative more than quantitative. External demand, most notably colonial demand, may have encouraged the utilization of underemployed or unemployed factors of production. Colonial demand for British manufactured goods may have been the extra demand pressure on scarce resources which forced new innovations. And long-distance trade with its risks and uncertainties encouraged institutional changes such as larger firm sizes and marine insurance, which in turn forced changes in capitalization and credit structures.[9] Fernand Braudel argues that long-distance trade concentrated profits in the hands of a few merchants. Thus, he states, "In the eighteenth century, one can undoubtedly say that <u>almost</u> everywhere in Europe, <u>large-scale</u> profits from trade were superior to <u>large-scale profits from industry or agriculture.</u>"[10] [Italics in the original] The commercial mechanism which accounted for much of this concentration of profits was the large joint-stock trading company, which Braudel concludes is among the best examples of merchant capitalism in early modern Europe, capitalism which was as sophisticated as later industrial capitalism.[11]

The joint-stock trading companies, such as the Hudson's Bay Company, emerged in northern Europe in the seventeenth century in response to the entrepreneurial problems posed by long-distance trade and colonial expansion.[12] While some would argue that they evolved naturally from the trading partnerships of medieval Italy, and presage the modern multinational corporation, this does not account adequately for their many mutations

---

[9]Jacob M. Price, "Colonial Trade and British Economic Development, 1660-1775" in <u>La Revolution américaine et L'Europe,</u> eds. Claude Fohlen and Jacques Godechot, Colloques internationaux du Centre National de la Recherche Scientifique, No. 577 (Paris: 1979), pp. 240-42.

[10]Fernand Braudel, <u>The Wheels of Commerce</u> (London: Collins, 1982), pp. 407, 428.

[11]Ibid., pp. 400-33.

[12]Barry Supple, "The Nature of Enterprise," in <u>The Economic Organization of Early Modern Europe</u>, pp. 439-45.

and regressions.[13]   Rather, the joint-stock trading company was one of the many organizational forms which Europeans devised to deal with the problems posed by expansion into non-European lands.[14] This expansion demanded larger and more speculative investments than had intra-European trade. Greater distances lengthened the turnover time of an investment and heightened the risks of piracy, shipwrecks, and wastage. Greater distances also lessened the reliability of the information needed to balance production with consumption and thereby increased investment risk and market uncertainty. Trading monopolies were one attempt to limit fluctuations in supply and demand.[15] Unlike the Spanish and Portuguese, who financed much of their initial expansion through state monopolies, the northern Europeans, especially the Dutch, English, and Danish, deviated from the Iberian example and financed their expansion through government chartered but privately financed joint-stock companies.[16]

In a signal work on the spice trade, Niels Steensgaard sought to explain the seventeenth-century eclipse of the Portuguese and Venetians by the Dutch and English. Not surprisingly, he originally attempted to determine whether the sea route around Africa, utilized by the Dutch and the English, was more profitable than the overland route across Asia to the Mediterranean. Discovering no significant cost advantage to either route, he concluded instead that the Dutch and English East India Companies differed fundamentally from the commercial organizations of the Portuguese and the Italians; the shift in commercial dominance from the Mediterranean to the North Atlantic can only be explained as a struc-

---

[13]See P. W. Klein, "The Origins of Trading Companies," in Companies and Trade, eds. L. Blusse and F. Gaastra (Leiden: Leiden University Press, 1981), pp. 17-28; and Niels Steensgaard, "The Companies as a Specific Institution in the History of European Expansion," in ibid., pp. 245-64, for arguments against this evolutionary model of joint-stock trading companies.

[14]Supple, "The Nature of Enterprise," p. 439.

[15]Ibid., p. 412.

[16]Ibid., p. 417; and Klein, "The Origins of Trading Companies," p. 25.

tural crisis.[17] By switching to the sea route the Dutch
and English companies internalized the protection costs
traditionally paid to rulers along the caravan routes,
and they sought to stabilize the violent fluctuations in
the market by institutionalizing controls on both the
prices and supply of goods. While these innovations did
not create greater profits, at least initially, they did
increase the amount of market information available to
the companies, making for greater market transparency[18]
and more efficient economic planning and control, thereby
better assuring the long-term survival of the companies.[19]

     Similarly, K. N. Chaudhuri, in a study of the English
East India Company from 1660-1760, maintains that the
"most difficult task for the ... managers was the creation of an economic decision-making process that would
establish equilibrium between the supply and the consum-
ing markets."[20] The East India Company minimized disequilibrium by constructing a managerial and administrative structure which systematized decision making and
established the operational parameters of the trade,
both at the sources of supply and the sources of demand.
From this structure, which differed radically from medieval and most other early modern trading partnerships in
Europe, the English East India Company derived its economic and political strength.[21] In Chaudhuri's opinion the

---

[17]Niels Steensgaard, Carracks, Caravans and Companies: The Structural Crisis in European-Asian Trade in
the Early Seventeenth Century (Odense, Denmark: Studentlitterature Andelsbogtrykkeriet, 1973), pp. 7, 10, 114.

[18]Market transparency refers to the amount of market
information known to the participants. Optimum market
transparency would involve full information on all market
variables, e.g., on production costs, overhead costs,
volume of supply, and level of demand. Long-distance
trade in the early modern period operated under conditions of poor market information and one of the challenges was to increase the level of information and make the
market more transparent.

[19]Steensgaard, Carracks, Caravans and Companies, pp.
11, 14-15, 47, 141-43.

[20]K. N. Chaudhuri, The Trading World of Asia and the
English East India Company, 1660-1760 (Cambridge: Cambridge University Press, 1978), p. 457.

[21]Ibid., pp. 19-22, 46, 457-58.

managers of the East India Company "had very little to learn from the modern system theorists."[22]

Historically, the distribution of investment risk has been considered the primary significance of the joint-stock company.[23] Pursuing this theme further, Steensgaard and Chaudhuri emphasize the ways in which the Dutch and English East India Companies evolved strategies for dealing with the market uncertainty in long-distance trade created by a lack of timely information to coordinate production and consumption, a problem which caused violent fluctuations in price and supply. In Steensgaard's words, "the companies transformed the gambler's profit of the long-distance trader into the safer, if less spectacular profit of conservative merchants."[24] Thus, a clue to understanding the economic power of trade is provided not through a simple examination of profits, but through an examination of the ability of firms to offset the uncertainty endemic in the seventeenth and eighteenth-century European economic world.[25]

The centralized administration of the Hudson's Bay Company and its preservation of most of its records makes it possible to analyze in detail the ways in which it coordinated the disparate spheres of its trade. The company's involvement in the London fur market, its procurement of trade goods, the trade in North America, and the interrelationship of the three will be considered here almost entirely from the perspective of the Committee in London which managed the company. Although this is a new approach to studying the Hudson's Bay Company and a refocusing of the European perspective it is not wholly divorced from previous work on the fur trade. A major issue in fur trade historiography has been the role

---

[22]K. N. Chaudhuri, "The English East India Company in the 17th and 18th Centuries: A Pre-Modern Multinational Organization," in Companies and Trade, p. 46.

[23] K. G. Davies, The Royal African Company (London: Longmans, Green & Co. Ltd., 1957), pp. 32-37.

[24]Steensgaard, "The Companies as a Specific Institution," p. 254.

[25]Supple, "The Nature of Enterprise," pp. 440-45; and Peter Musgrave, "The Economics of Uncertainty: The Structural Revolution in the Spice Trade, 1480-1640," in Shipping, Trade, and Commerce, eds. P. L. Cottrell and D. H. Aldcroft (Leicester: Leicester University Press, 1981) pp. 9-21.

of the trade in the expansion of European civilization
across North America, and the rivalry over who would
control the continent. Harold Innis argued that the
eventual elimination of the French in the Canadian fur
trade was due to cheaper and better English trade goods
and the shorter route to the fur-rich interior through
Hudson Bay rather than the St. Lawrence River-Great Lakes
route.[26] William Eccles in a "belated review" of Innis'
work contends that after the decline of beaver prices at
the end of the seventeenth century the fur trade became a
matter of imperial strategy, at which the French excelled
to the detriment of the English.[27] These analyses have
been presented in terms of the imperial and mercantile
policies of the European actors, with less attention
given to the specific commercial structures which sus-
tained that expansion. This study seeks to balance that
approach with an emphasis on the commercial organization
of the Hudson's Bay Company.

---

[26]Harold A. Innis, The Fur Trade in Canada, rev. ed.
(Toronto: University of Toronto Press, 1956), pp. 47-49,
52, 78-80, 82-83, 144, 391.

[27]W. J. Eccles, "Belated review of Harold Adams
Innis, The Fur Trade in Canada" Canadian Historical
Review 60, no. 1 (1979): 419-41.

Chapter I

COLONIZATION OR COMMERCE? PATTERNS OF EXPANSION

The unequalled longevity of the Hudson's Bay Company among European trading companies belies its commonplace beginnings. It was only one of the many maritime companies which Europeans established during the seventeenth century for discovery, commerce, and colonization. Most collapsed after a few voyages; founders lost their investments and trading generally witnessed a return to individually owned firms or small partnerships. Patterns of company success do emerge though. The Dutch and English East India Companies demonstrated the viability of company trading in Asia. In the Atlantic sphere there were no parallels to the East India Companies in terms of size and power; of the dozens of English companies chartered to trade to the Americas and Africa only the Hudson's Bay Company and the Royal African Company proved commercially viable. The other Atlantic companies founded by the Dutch, French, Danish, Portuguese, and Spanish fared no better than most of the English.[28]

The persistence of the Hudson's Bay Company in the New World when other companies perished, most in their infancy, has been attributed by Niels Steensgaard to its chartered status, to geographic conditions which made colonization difficult, and to the specialized nature of its trade.[29] But to credit the company's success to these external circumstances would imply that internal factors of organization (the ability to maximize opportunities and minimize risk) were largely insignificant to its successful prosecution of trade. Positive circumstances can be offset by external disruptions such as war, natural disaster, currency

_____

[28]See Niels Steensgaard, "The Companies as a Specific Institution in the History of European Expansion," in Companies and Trade, eds. L. Blusse and F. Gaastra (Leiden: Leiden University Press, 1981), pp. 251-60 for a discussion of the differences between company trade in Asia and the Atlantic.

[29]Ibid., p. 258.

9

fluctuations, or changes in the market; and internal
organization becomes a crucial factor in determining
whether a business can withstand external economic
tremblings. In the case of the Hudson's Bay Company,
entrepreneurial innovation and rationalization resulted
in the development of a managerial and administrative
structure capable of coordinating the disparate spheres
of its trade, separated one from the other by time,
space, and culture. This managerial and administrative
development must account, in part, for the transition of
the Hudson's Bay Company from a highly speculative
seventeenth-century venture with colonial intentions to
an eighteenth-century gilt-edged trading company.

The men who founded the Hudson's Bay Company enter-
tained virtually every expansionistic aspiration that a
seventeenth-century European could imagine. Hopes for
finding the fabled Northwest Passage to the South Seas
were renewed, trading possibilities appeared legion,
mines would yield "Gold Silver Gemms and Precious
Stones," and "Castles Fortificacions Fortes Garrisons
Colonyes...Plantacions Townes or Villages" would dot the
landscape.[30] Some of the expectations expounded in the
charter were the stock litany of adventurers hedging
their bets in their contract with the Crown. But high
hopes and blindly extravagant romanticism were the opium
of the adventurer's pipe dreams. From the haze envelop-
ing the promoters of the Hudson's Bay Company only one
dream, the fur trade, became a reality and it alone led
to a permanent European presence in the Canadian North.
Experience disabused dreamers of realizing their other
aspirations, at least for a century and a half.[31]

The harshness of the country named Rupert's Land
exceeded the expectations of the men who founded the
Hudson's Bay Company, despite the discouraging reports
brought back by early explorers. From 1550 onwards, a
quixotic search for the fabled Northwest Passage to
Cathay had led Europeans to explore the arctic, first
along the coast of Scandinavia and Russia, then westwards
to Greenland and the northeast coast of North America.

---

[30]"The Royal Charter Incorporating The Hudson's Bay
Company, A.D. 1670," rpt. in Minutes of the Hudson's Bay
Company, 1671-1674, ed. E. E. Rich, (London: Hudson's
Bay Record Society, vol. 5, 1942), pp. 131, 139, 145.

[31]In 1811, 140 years after the chartering of the
Hudson's Bay Company, Lord Selkirk sponsored the Red
River settlement, the first European agricultural
settlement in Rupert's Land.

In 1610 Henry Hudson became the first European to enter the inland sea which bears his name. Trapped in the ice-locked bay, Hudson wintered on James Bay, only to be left to perish by a mutinous crew the following spring. In 1612 two of that crew again sailed for Hudson Bay, this time led by Thomas Button. English merchants financed another two voyages that same decade under the commands of Robert Bylot and William Baffin. In 1619 the Danish Crown sent out Jens Munk to try his hand at finding the illusory Northwest Passage. The autumn onset of winter in the bay caught Munk unawares, forcing him to establish winter quarters at Churchill River. The following spring he and the two surviving members of his crew of sixty-four returned to Denmark. Word of the horror of Munk's voyage quickly spread among Danish sailors, none of whom would volunteer for a second Danish voyage to the harsh and unmerciful Hudson Bay. The English, yet undeterred, funded two more voyages, both of which sailed in 1630.[32] Despite these repeated efforts no voyage to Hudson Bay produced anything save an enlarged knowledge of the world. No one discovered prospects of trade, of land to settle, or of a passage to the Orient that would prompt Europeans to return annually or settle permanently.

London merchants had funded most of the early and fruitless voyages to Hudson Bay and it is therefore not surprising that in 1666, when two Frenchmen, Pierre Radisson and Medard Chouart, Sieur des Groseilliers, came to town with a tale about furs from Hudson Bay, merchants had few pounds to spare to finance a voyage to verify the story. A group of Restoration courtiers, however, smitten by the tale, assembled the necessary resources to outfit two ships. One of the two, the Nonsuch, completed the voyage in 1669, returning to London with a cargo of furs worth £1379.6s.10d, probably not enough to cover the expenses involved, but the first marketable goods to be brought from Hudson Bay.[33] The safe homecoming of the Nonsuch buoyed the spirits of the organizers, but it would be erroneous to conclude that their primary intention was to pursue the fur trade for its own ends. Furs guaranteed income, the income necessary to sustain an

---

[32]E. E. Rich, Hudson's Bay Company, 1670-1870, vol. 1: 1670-1673 (London: Hudson's Bay Record Society, 1958), pp. 6-7; J. H. Parry, The Age of Reconnaissance (New York: Mentor Books, 1963), pp. 221-22; and W. A. Kenyon, ed. and intro. The Journal of Jens Munk, 1619-1620 (Toronto: Royal Ontario Museum, 1980), pp. vii-xiii.

[33]E. E. Rich, Hudson's Bay Company, 1670-1870, vol. 1, pp. 29-30, 42.

expansionistic venture over an extended period. The
wording of the charter, the composition of the initial
shareholders, the early organization of the company, and
the economic function of the fur trade in other North
American colonies suggest that the promoters intended the
fur trade to finance other avenues of development in
Hudson Bay.

Despite numerous voyages of discovery the land around
Hudson Bay remained unclaimed until the establishment of
trading posts by the Hudson's Bay Company. English
custom held that European claims to the non-Christian
world had to be legitimized with permanent settlements.[34]
Where Europeans did settle permanently they adopted one
of two principal forms. The first included trading sta-
tions, forts, and factories, settlements designed to
facilitate trading voyages and to validate European claim
and presence. Settlement was permanent, but settlers
were for the most part impermanent, employees of a company stationed at a post for a number of years before
being transferred, sent home, or quitting employment.
These settlements were essentially company towns, charac-
teristic of most European settlements in Asia and Africa.
Only gradually did enclaves of permanent European settlers emerge. Most settlements in the Americas were, in
contrast, of the more familiar second type: communities
of permanent settlers.

Economics was a major determinant of this difference
in settlement patterns. Europeans had been trading with
Asians for centuries before the Portuguese rounded the
Cape of Good Hope or the powerful East India Companies
were established. The rapid growth of European trade
with Asia in the sixteenth and seventeenth centuries was
founded upon well-established patterns of commerce, and
depended on the highly stratified and sophisticated
social, political, and economic systems of Asian socie-
ties. An Asian labor force organized and controlled by
Asians produced the goods which Europeans wanted. For
many years Europeans functioned only as merchants, pro-
viding the link between Asian suppliers and the European
market. Europeans operated much the same way in the
slave trade; African slavers amassed the slaves which
Europeans then bought, transported, and sold on the slave
markets in the Americas. In this type of trade, where
the merchant trader was the one necessary link between
sources of demand and sources of supply, permanent

---

[34]Kenneth G. Davies, The North Atlantic World in the
Seventeenth Century (Minneapolis: University of Minn-
esota Press, 1974), p. 36.

settlements of impermanent settlers met both the commercial and strategic requirements of European expansion.[35]

The American trades required more economic links for getting products from the Americas to the European market and thus presented greater problems of organization than existed in the Asian or African trade. The commodities which the Americas promised and Europe desired, sugar, tobacco, cocoa, indigo, fish, and timber, were not produced in marketable quantities by indigenous Americans. Therefore, Europeans had to commit themselves intensively and extensively to the Americas if they were to derive riches from the continents. Two fundamental transformations were required. The New World's landscape had to be redesigned for the cultivation of surplus agricultural products and a labor supply had to be found. Indigenous Americans resisted bonding their labor to Europeans and hence labor was imported: settlers and indentured labor from Europe; enslaved labor from Africa.[36] One notable exception to this pattern in North America was the fur trade, in which the Indians controlled the production of furs and Europeans served almost solely as traders. The Hudson Bay fur trade broke the New World pattern of permanent settlement with permanent settlers, though not without a reconceptualization of the European attitude that in the Americas commerce and colonization were flipsides of the same coin.

In the British American colonies along the eastern seaboard, fur became an immediate "cash crop" marketable in Europe in exchange for the few manufactures required by the settlers. The trade allowed settlers to pursue other economic ends: mixed farming for New Englanders; a tobacco economy in the Chesapeake. In New France, New Netherlands, and Nova Scotia a greater tension marked the process of reconciling whether the fur trade would be the raison d'etre of settlement, or whether it would be the major economic underpinning of a larger colonial en-

---

[35]Kenneth G. Davies, Royal African Company (London: Longmans, Green & Co., Ltd., 1957), pp. 3-4; and Steensgaard, "The Companies as a Specific Institution," p. 253.

[36]E. E. Rich, "Colonial Settlement and Its Labour Problems" in The Economy of Expanding Europe in the 16th and 17th Centuries, vol. 4, Cambridge Economic History of Europe, eds. E. E. Rich and C. H. Wilson (Cambridge University Press, 1967), pp. 302-73.

deavor.[37]   Similarly, the promoters of the Hudson's Bay
Company anticipated and planned for colonization to
follow on the heels of the fur trade.   That it came to
resemble the organization and settlement patterns of the
Asian and African trades was coincidence, not design.

The promoters of expansionistic ventures did not plan
their undertakings recklessly or uncritically, though in
most cases their original formulations were unachieved.
The founding of three companies, the Company of Royal
Adventurers Trading into Africa in 1663, the Carolina
Company in 1663, and the Hudson's Bay Company in 1670,
illustrates this deliberateness.   All three shared as
principal promoters a group of courtiers influential in
the Restoration Court and intent upon territorial and
economic jockeying with European rivals.   The Company of
Royal Adventurers into Africa was to counter the Dutch
and Portuguese control of the slave trade.   Settlement in
the Carolinas would extend English presence south of
Virginia and block Spanish settlement north of Florida.
The Hudson's Bay Company would flank French Canada on the
north, complementing recently won New York on the south,
and both would help undercut the French dominance of the
fur trade.   The intended means for achieving these similar imperial ends differed significantly among the three
companies despite their shared promoters.   The charter of
the Royal Adventurers contained almost solely provisions
for trade, although like other charters for trade to non-
Christian lands it allowed for the establishment of
factories and trading posts.[38]   The charter of the Carolina Company named eight men, who received the right to
plant a proprietary colony for agricultural development.

---

[37]E. E. Rich, Hudson's Bay Company, 1670-1870, vol.
1, pp. 8, 12-13, 45-46; John G. Reid, Acadia, Maine and
New Scotland (Toronto: University of Toronto Press,
1981), pp. 19-20; and Van Cleaf Bachman, Peltries or
Plantations: The Economic Policies of the Dutch West
India Company in New Netherland, 1623-1639 (Baltimore:
Johns Hopkins University Press, 1969), passim.

[38]Reprints of the charters for the Company of Royal
Adventurers Into Africa and the Royal African Company can
be found in Selected Charters of Trading Companies, A. D.
1530-1707, ed. Cecil T. Carr, (1913; rpt. New York: Burt
Franklin, 1970), pp. 172-77, 177-81, 186-92.   A short
discussion of the African companies is in the introduction, pp. xliii-xlviii.   See also Davies, Royal African
Company, pp. 36-37, 97-99; and David W. Galenson, Traders, Planters, and Slaves: Market Behavior in Early
English America (Cambridge University Press, 1986).

This charter for colonization contained specific details on land tenure and the establishment of civil governance.[39]   The Hudson's Bay Company charter fell between the other two. It prescribed guidelines for establishing permanent and abiding settlements and civil governance, as well as trading privileges and the means of subcontracting those trading privileges to settlers.[40]

Of the three, only the Hudson's Bay Company survived as a chartered concern. In 1672 the Company of Royal Adventurers Trading into Africa reorganized itself as the Royal Africa Company. With the change came a marked transition in the composition of the shareholders from primarily peers to merchants and City men. The company lost its monopoly in 1712-13, and then dissolved in 1752, never having distributed regular dividends. Planned as a colonizing venture, the Carolina Company hoped to profit from proprietary rents, without having to invest heavily in settlements. After nearly collapsing during its early years, the project regained vigor through the exertions of Sir Anthony Ashley Cooper, Earl of Shaftesbury, and more generous financing by the proprietors. But political factions within the Carolinas, Indian wars, and the proprietors' increasing disinterest in the management of a venture which promised few pecuniary returns, led to the overthrow of the proprietary government in 1719. Time and experience led the Hudson's Bay Company to concentrate on the fur trade while at the same time muting its egregiously misguided colonial ambitions. Nevertheless, for nearly thirty years the company labored under the illusion that colonies along Hudson Bay were tenable and desirable. Variations in the initial organization and structure of the Royal Adventurers, the Carolina Company, and the Hudson's Bay Company indicate

---

[39]The charter for the Carolina Company can be found in The Federal and State Constitutions, Colonial Charters, and Other Organic Laws of the States, Territories, and Colonies Now or Heretofore Forming the United States of America, vol. 5, ed. Francis Newton Thrope, (Washington: Government Printing Office, 1909), pp. 2743-53. For a discussion of the founding of the company and its subsequent collapse see M. Eugene Sirmans, Colonial South Carolina: A Political History, 1663-1763 (Chapel Hill: University of North Carolina Press, 1966) pp. 3-128.

[40]The Charter for the Hudson's Bay Company can be found in Appendix A of Minutes of the Hudson's Bay Company, 1671-1674, pp. 131-48. See also Rich, Hudson's Bay Company, 1670-1870, vol. 1, pp. 52-60; and Carr, Selected Charters, pp. lxxxix-xc.

that promoters of these ventures did attempt to tailor
them to perceived possibilities. Thus, it is historically significant that the founders of the Hudson's Bay
Company originally envisioned their enterprise as very
different from that which ultimately developed.

The company's determination to plant a colony waxed
and waned. Early on the Committee in London, the elected
committee of shareholders that managed the company, toyed
with the idea of sending men and building supplies to
begin a settlement. In January 1672 they discussed
sending two ships and hiring thirty men "for Stayeing in
the Countrey." By February the head-count fell to twenty-
five men, and by April to fifteen.[41] It is unclear
whether the reductions were for reasons of cost or because few men could be persuaded to sign on. The first
bayside governor seems to have been chosen with a view to
governing a colony rather than managing trade, as the
Quaker Charles Bayly never exhibited business acumen but
did foster amiable relations with the Indians.[42] The
company replaced him in 1674, probably because of his
business shortcomings, with William Lydall, "who hath
made many Voyages to and from Russia and Lived many
yeares therein."[43] James Bay was not Russia, and after
one sorry winter Lydall returned to London and Bayly
resumed command.[44] In 1679 the company recalled Bayly
and replaced him with John Nixon, formerly in the employ
of the East India Company, a sign that the company
intended to give more attention to matters of trade.[45]

For the next twenty years the company intermittently
instructed the traders on measures to be taken to prepare
for settlers. In 1683 Henry Sergeant went to James Bay
as governor, taking along his wife, her maid, and a

---

[41]Minutes, 16 January 1671/2; 1 February 1671/2; and
17 April 1672; in Rich, Minutes, 1671-1674, pp. 19, 22,
35-36.

[42]Rich, H.B.C., 1670-1870, vol. 1, pp. 67, 80.

[43]Minutes, 29 January 1673/4, in Rich, Minutes,
1671-1674, p. 74.

[44]Rich, H.B.C., 1670-1870, vol. 1, p. 79.

[45]E. E. Rich, Minutes of the Hudson's Bay Company,
1679-1684, (London: Hudson's Bay Record Society, vol. 8,
1945), pp. 252-53.

clergyman.[46] The committee advised him to have the men
engage "either in cultivateing the land, in fishing and
in makeing oyle, or in makeing pott ashes or else you
may judge for the service of the Company, we intending as
soone as may be to plant a Colloney there."[47] It urged
Sergeant, as it had his predecessors, to apply his "ut-
most skill and industrey" to lessening the costs of
provisioning the post. To this end it included in the
1683 shipment "severall sorts of seeds and graynes."[48]
In 1684 the company sent to Norway for two goats to ship
to the bay.[49] In the view of the committee the creation
of a pastoral life on the shores of Hudson Bay was possible. In 1692 it pleaded with George Geyer, governor at
York Fort, to remain another year. Not only, it reasoned,
would it be in the company's interest, but it would allow
Geyer to "have the honour and satisfaction you seeke, of
Leaving that Trade which you enlarged, that Building
which you have erected, that Vineyard which you have
Planted, in Peaceable and florishing Condition, and out
of danger of being undermined by the Foxes, or destroyed
by the Wild Boares of the Forrest."[50] Geyer remained at
York Fort, but presumably not to refine the pastoral
life. The Committee in London, however, thought he
should be about the task and the following year it sent
elaborate instructions on how to prepare York Fort for
the arrival of cattle. A barn was to have been built to
stable sixteen to eighteen head of cattle, hay gathered,
and the Indians encouraged to kill "wolves and Revenous
beasts" in the area. The committee, likely swayed by
Samuel Clarke, its deputy governor, "whoe hath lived 20
years in Cold Counteryes," was convinced that the plan
was feasible "for Findland and Lapland are Cold and
colder and more barren and unfrutfull and much Longer

---

[46]Letter Outward (hereafter L.O.) to Henry Sergeant,
16 May 1684, in Letters Outward, 1679-1694, ed. E. E.
Rich (London: Hudson's Bay Record Society, vol. 11,
1948), p. 120.

[47]L.O. to Henry Sergeant, 27 April 1683, Letters
Outward, vol. 11, pp. 76-77.

[48]Ibid., p. 77.

[49]Minutes, 16 May 1685, Hudson's Bay Company Archives, Provincial Archives of Manitoba, A.1/8, fo. 32d.
(Hereafter only the HBCA classification number is given.)

[50]L.O. to Geyer, 17 June 1692, in Letters Outward,
1688-1696, ed. E. E. Rich (London: Hudson's Bay Record
Society, vol. 20, 1957), p. 140.

Nights then at Yorke fort and yett at those places Cat-
tell are maintained."   The committee did qualify its
instructions telling Geyer that if he found "upon mature
deliberation the climate alltogether imposeble for their
[the cattles'] Subsistance" the plan for raising them
would be rethought.[51]

Horticulture was not to be neglected at York Fort and
seeds, farm implements, and a book on gardening were
included in the 1693 shipment.   To make the seeds grow to
perfection, the men should "raise a heighth of Ground or
Hedge of reeds or some fence to keep the Norwest wind
from them, and then there is now [no] Doubt of their
comming to p[er]fection as well as in any pte. of Sweeden
and Norway."[52]   At more southerly James Bay horticulture
was pursued with marginally more success than at York
Fort.   The committee, hoping to capitalize on the prospects, decided that flax might be commercially grown.   In
the letter giving instructions for growing flax, the
committee retracted the plan, not because of the climate
or geographic conditions, but because it took skilled
labor to harvest and process flax.[53]   While the bayside
posts did maintain kitchen gardens and some livestock,
especially at Albany Fort on James Bay, nothing approach-
ing concentrated farming ever developed.[54]

The slowness with which the shareholders of the company surrendered their visions of bucolic life on Hudson
Bay to the reality of the subarctic was only exceeded by
their slowness in accepting the fact that virtually the
only marketable products available were furs.   Annual
admonitions from London suggested that the men were
giving insufficient attention to diversifying the trade.
Mining was recurringly thought to be potentially profitable.   In 1682 the company sent out George Geyer to
develop the mining of isinglass, a contemporary term for
the mineral mica, and in 1684 Sergeant was ordered to
send ten men to East Main, on the east shore of James

[51]L.O. to Geyer, 17 June 1693, ibid., pp. 192, 194-5.

[52]Ibid., pp. 195-96.

[53]L.O. to Knight, 30 May 1698, ibid., pp. 272, 274.

[54]Richard Glover, intro., Letters from Hudson Bay,
1703-40, ed. K. G. Davies (London: Hudson's Bay Record
Society, vol. 25, 1965), p. xxi.

Bay, to settle it for the isinglass trade.[55] Minerals, the committee explained to Thomas Walsh, governor at York Fort, "are easily found by the Couler of the water that owzeth or springeth out of the earth where they are being of a Brownish Coulor some what enclineing to blew or seeming Greasy, which must be traced to the head of the spring, Copper mines the water green and Greasey."[56] Whaling also seemed worth pursuing. Geyer had orders to send men to Churchill River, north of York Fort, to establish a whaling station. The committee would suffer no excuses for his not proceeding on the orders, noting that "Capt. Young tho never in Greenland in his life, for the time he was in Churchill River he struck and took as many Whales as the Harponier, that we gave double wages, and soe did some of his men ... for its a slight of hand and noe great art ... all the men delight in taking them making it a sport and not a Labor or toyle."[57]

Some of the envisioned expansion of the trade involved having the Indians diversify the goods they brought to trade. Among other items, the committee suggested goose feathers, castoreum, and seahorse teeth (walrus tusks), but despite all the efforts nothing further developed. Over a number of years cargoes of feathers, castoreum or ivory would make it to London, but they met with mixed market success. The company received castoreum regularly from 1688 to 1718, and then received no castoreum until sometime after 1729.[58] A 280-pound shipment of castoreum was sent to Amsterdam in 1698 because it would not sell in London.[59] After a few bundles of quills reached London in the 1720s the committee advised the traders not to send any more as there was no market for them.[60]

The reliance of the Hudson's Bay Company on furs, especially beaver, caused some concern. Many of the committee's exhortations to diversify the trade were

---

[55]L.O. to Sergeant, 16 May 1684, Letters Outward, vol. 11, pp. 121-22.

[56]L.O. to Walsh, 30 May 1694, Letters Outward, vol. 20, p. 237.

[57]L.O. to Geyer, 17 June 1693, ibid., pp. 187-88.

[58]See Appendix for data and citations for the cargoes from the bay from 1681 to 1729.

[59]Journal of Foreign Accounting, A.17/1, fo. 42.

[60]L.O. to McCliesh, 28 May 1723, A.6/4, fo. 72d.

uttered with the hope of lessening the dependence on beaver. What significant diversification did occur was in small luxury furs such as fox, otter, and particularly marten.[61] After the Treaty of Utrecht in 1713, when James Knight returned to the bay to supplant the French traders at York, the committee encouraged him to pursue the possibility of copper mining or trade as "it would turn to better accompt than Skins."[62] Thus as late as 1715 the company still sought other areas of trade, rather than relying primarily on furs.

Examination of the early goals of the Hudson's Bay Company suggests that external conditions, not an exaggerated belief in the profitability of the fur trade, determined its singular reliance on fur. Geography and climate created inflexible constraints within which the company had to operate. Ironically, those limitations probably increased the likelihood of the company's survival during its first century. Climate precluded agricultural settlement along the bay and thereby a population which would probably have challenged the company's hegemony as had happened elsewhere in North America, and as indeed occurred in southern Manitoba after the founding of the Red River settlement in the early nineteenth century.[63] Lack of avenues for economic expansion into areas like mining had the positive effect of keeping the company's labor force small, specialized, and manageable. The harshness of the Canadian subarctic also discouraged challengers. Therefore the constraints imposed by environmental conditions had some positive effects. They were not, however, sufficient to offset the fickleness and vicissitudes of long-distance trade during this period. Management and administration

---

[61]Small furs did play an important part in the fortunes of the company. For the period 1738-63 see Arthur J. Ray, "Buying and Selling Hudson's Bay Company Furs in the Eighteenth Century," in Explorations in Canadian Economic History: Essays in Honour of Irene M. Spry, ed. Duncan Cameron (Ottawa: University of Ottawa Press, 1985), pp. 95-115.

[62]L.O. to Knight, 31 May 1717, A.6/4, fo. 12.

[63]For a revisionist interpretation see D. W. Moodie, "Agriculture and the Fur Trade," in Old Trails and New Directions: Papers of the Third North American Fur Trade Conference, eds. Carol M. Judd and Arthur J. Ray (University of Toronto Press, 1980), 272-90 in which he argues that the view that agriculture and the fur trade were incompatible needs serious qualification.

remained crucial components in the explanation of the survival of the Hudson's Bay Company.

Chapter 2

THE HUDSON'S BAY COMPANY

AND THE ENGLISH FUR MARKET, 1670-1726

In 1669 the first shipment of furs from Hudson Bay signalled the possibility of a significant new fur supply
for a market already in transition.   Only two years
before, with the Treaty of Breda, the Dutch had relin-
quished to the English their claim to New Netherlands
(renamed New York) and with it the sizeable fur trade of
the Hudson River and its hinterland.   Prior to 1667 a
modest but steady stream of furs had been coming into
England from New England, Virginia, and Maryland, but its
volume was far less than the potential of either the
Hudson River or Hudson Bay trade.   The nearly simultaneous acquisition of New York and Hudson Bay by the
English had a twofold impact on the European fur market.
On the one hand furs from New York now went into London
rather than Amsterdam.   The Dutch, though losing their
direct supply of North American furs, nevertheless still
dominated Baltic shipping and served as middlemen in the
beaver trade with Russia.   On the other hand the English
suddenly had two new substantial supplies of furs which
either had to be absorbed into the domestic market or re-
exported to other parts of Europe.   Moreover, a growing
volume of furs from New France was saturating the continental market.   By 1690 the European market was flooded
with beaver and fur prices began to decline.

The oversupply of beaver and the resultant fall in
prices in the late seventeenth century mirror a market
phenomenon associated with nearly every commodity of
long-distance trade in the seventeenth and eighteenth
centuries.   In 1639 an over-production of tobacco caused
prices to slump.   French and English growers on St. Kitts
agreed not to plant tobacco for a year.   Virginia placed
a 1,500,000 pound ceiling on 1639 production and for the
following two years a 1,200,000 pound ceiling.   In 1650
tea in England sold from between £6 and £10 per pound.
By 1703 the price had sunk to sixteen shillings per
pound.   When sugar production on the West Indian islands
of Martinique and Guadeloupe came onstream, raw sugar

prices dropped by nearly fifty percent.[64]   As new colonial commodities were introduced they commanded high prices and encouraged the entry of new producers. Production would soon exceed demand and prices would drop.   Eventually prices would stabilize at a new low level and thereafter would move in relation to price trends in Europe.[65]

Increasing supply and dropping prices often resulted in expanded consumption, but it also wreaked havoc for many merchants. W. J. Eccles has argued that after the drop in beaver prices in the 1690s the Canadian beaver trade was not economically viable, but that the French government maintained it for imperial and military purposes.[66]   In contrast to his picture of New France, the Hudson's Bay Company, operating under the protection of a government charter yet not with direct financial backing from the government, emerged in the first half of the eighteenth century as a profit-making enterprise, despite the difficult two decades from 1690 to 1710.   For the Hudson's Bay Company the decline in beaver prices in the 1690s did not herald the crippling of a previously thriving commercial enterprise; though for the most part healthy, the Hudson's Bay Company was yet a struggling youngster in 1690.   Optimism and high beaver prices, not financial stability, account for the four dividends distributed in 1684, 1688, 1689, and 1690, the only ones paid between 1670 and 1718.[67]   The recovery of the Hudson's Bay Company and its commencement of annual dividends in 1718 thus stand in contrast to the picture drawn of the French trade.

---

[64]G. B. Masefield, "Crops and Livestock," in The Economy of Expanding Europe in the Sixteenth Century, vol. 4, Cambridge Economic History of Europe, eds. E. E. Rich and C. H. Wilson (Cambridge: Cambridge University Press, 1967), pp. 287, 289, 291, 294, 298.

[65]John J. McCusker and Russell R. Menard, The Economy of British America, 1607-1789 (Chapel Hill and London: University of North Carolina Press, 1985), p. 67.

[66]W. J. Eccles, "The Fur Trade and Eighteenth-Century Imperialism," William and Mary Quarterly, 3d. ser. 15, no. 3 (1983), 341-42, 344; W. J. Eccles, "A Belated Review of Harold Adams Innis, The Fur Trade in Canada," Canadian Historical Review, 60, no. 4 (1979), 422-23.

[67]K. G. Davies, "The Years of No Dividends: Finances of the Hudson's Bay Company, 1690-1718," in People and Pelts, ed. Malvina Bolus (Winnipeg: Peguis, 1972), p. 67.

The survival of the Hudson's Bay Company is partly attributable to the willingness of the shareholders to forego dividends.[68]   What previous studies have not accounted for, however, is what happened to beaver prices after their collapse in 1690, and the commercial responses of the various participants in the fur trade.   The purpose of this chapter is to explore the participation of the Hudson's Bay Company in the European fur market from 1670 to 1726.   This time span encompasses the shaky beginnings of the company, the ebullient years when the first dividends were distributed, the years of a depressed fur market and no dividends, the Anglo-French conflicts which ended with the Treaty of Utrecht in 1713, and finally the period of a stabilized trade with regular dividends.   Three major areas will be considered: one, the company's use of its charter to restrict and influence the trade; two, the importance the company placed on market information and the role of that information in its decision-making; and, three, the prices the company received for its furs and the volume of furs it imported into England.   These factors will suggest some of the ways in which the company managed its affairs to cope with the vicissitudes of long-distance trade.

One of the privileges granted a chartered company was control over the trade to, from, and within the area defined by its charter.   However, most of the companies which intended to bring in colonists, as the Hudson's Bay Company first planned, included clauses for sub-contracting trading rights.[69]   The Hudson's Bay Company charter reads:

> Wee streightly Charge Command and prohibite for us our heirs and successors ... that none of them directly or indirectly doe visit haunt frequent or Trade Trafficke or Adventure by way of Merchandize into or from any the said Territoryes Lymittes or Places ... <u>unlesse itt bee by the Lycence and agreement of the said Governor and Company</u> in writing first had and obteyned under theire Common Seale...[70] [emphasis added]

---

[68]Ibid., passim.

[69]E. E. Rich, <u>Hudson's Bay Company, 1670-1870</u>, vol. 1: <u>1670-1763</u> (London: Hudson's Bay Record Society, 1958), p. 55.

[70]Royal Charter, 1670, rpt. in <u>Minutes of the Hudson's Bay Company, 1671-1674</u>, ed. E. E. Rich (London: Hudson's Bay Record Society, vol. 5, 1942), p. 142.

Initially the company appears to have allowed some private trade by ships' captains and by their first governor at the bay, Charles Bayly, but by 1673 the committee in London was authorizing searches of the ships to look for smuggled furs.[71] Despite repeated prohibitions on private trade the practice persisted and the company sought efficacious ways to stop it. In the 1683 annual letter to the bay the committee instructed Governor John Bridgar to administer an oath to all officers forswearing private trade "which by the Tenor of our Charter you have the power to administer."[72] Afterwards he was to notify the committee of the names of the men who had taken the oath. Before the sailing of the ship from England the committee had the ships' captains and officers take a similar oath, and some protested vociferously at the restraints the company tried to place on them.[73] During the tenure of Governor John Nixon at the bay, ships' captains had been given beaver coats. In 1685 Governor Henry Sergeant was ordered to stop the practice, "for under the Colour of such presents they frequently conveigh away severall other Furrs."[74] Private trade continued. In 1686 the committee sent messages to Captains Robert Porten, John Outlaw, and William Bond telling them that Mr. Morgan Lodge had been retained by the company to board their ships and search for smuggled furs. If Mr. Lodge discovered clandestine trade the committee would "proceed against every one we find culpable."[75] Private trade never went away entirely, but was checked for a while, for when the committee contracted for Mr. Lodge's services in 1693, it remarked that it had

---

[71]Minutes, 13 October 1673, ibid., p. 51.

[72]Letter Outward (hereafer L.O.) to John Bridgar, 27 April 1683, in Letters Outward, 1679-1694, ed. E. E. Rich (London: Hudson's Bay Record Society, vol. 11, 1948), p. 88.

[73]Minutes, 28 May 1682, in Minutes of the Hudson's Bay Company, 1679-1684, ed. E. E. Rich (London: Hudson's Bay Record Society, vol. 8, 1945), p. 228.

[74]L.O. to Henry Sergeant, 22 May 1685, in Letters Outward, vol. 11, p. 142.

[75]L.O. to Capt. William Bond, 6 October 1686; and L.O. to Mr. Morgan Lodge, 6 October 1686, ibid., p. 203.

"not of Late had ocasion to Trouble you."[76]   Nevertheless, "great Quantities of Castorium and Furrs" still
came in as private trade that year.[77]

    The limits to which the company would enforce restric-
tions on private trade and interlopers varied from year
to year, largely depending on how it and its challengers
chose to interpret the charter. The letter outward in
1682 alerted the Council at Albany River to rumors that
former employees of the company were designing interlop-
ing voyages to Hudson Bay. The council was to seize
English ships sailing into the bay and have them sent
back to England for prosecution. Foreign ships could be
seized as "lawful prize pursuant to the Act of Parliament
for the Encouragemt. of Navigation." At the end of the
letter, however, the committee appended instructions to
John Nixon, the governor, negating the preceding order.
"Yet being further Sensible of the greate Contempt such
person will offer to his Majesties Gratious Pattent
granted this Company Have thought fit to take this matter
into further Consideration."[78]   Back in London the
company had problems of its own, including the threat of
challenges to its charter[79] and an undefined legal battle
brought against it by Captain Greenway, formerly in its
employ.[80] These events probably explain the instructions
to Nixon to act discreetly and cautiously with interlopers.

    The logistical difficulty of maintaining a viable
trade over great distances occasionally created problems
for the regulation of private trade. In 1681 trade goods
ran low at the bay and Governor Nixon allowed the men at
the fort and on the ships to trade their blankets and
clothes with the Indians so as not to have to refuse the
furs they had brought to trade. When the ships returned
to England in October of that year many of the furs on
board belonged to the men. The committee ordered them to

----

[76]L.O. to Mr. Morgan Lodge, 14 November 1693, in
Letters Outward, 1688-1696, ed. E. E. Rich (London:
Hudson's Bay Record Society, vol. 20, 1957), p. 226.

    [77]L.O. to Walsh, 3 June 1694, in ibid., pp. 238-39.

    [78]L.O. to Nixon, 22 May 1682, in Letters Outward,
vol. 11, pp. 46-47.

    [79]Rich, H.B.C., 1670-1870, vol. 1, pp. 102-3.

    [80]From the minutes, in Minutes, 1679-1684 vol. 8,
pp. 161, 166, 172, 178, 180, 195, 201.

be seized and taken to the company's warehouse, and
declared that the men would be reimbursed in money.[81] On
December 9 the committee had the furs transported to
committeeman John Letton's house to be sold and the pro-
ceeds were to have been divided equitably among the men
who owned the furs.[82] By December 14 the committee had
agreed to return the dressed moose skins but still insis-
ted on selling the furs, and two days later they were to
be put on display for prospective buyers.[83] Between then
and January 5 something transpired which made the committee change its mind and allow the owners to come and
reclaim their furs.[84] There is no hint about why the
original decision was reversed but the incident surely
impressed upon the company the necessity of not skimping
in the quantity of trade goods, and illustrates the
dilemmas created when others stepped in to fill the void.
In its letter to Nixon the following spring the committee
told him it had returned the furs to their respective
owners as he had requested in his letter, but that hence-
forth if the situation arose again the company would
seize all furs as rightfully belonging to it.[85]

The monopoly status which the company enjoyed was a
highly qualified one. In Hudson Bay and its hinterland
the charter supposedly protected the company from compet-
ing with its own nationals, but there remained the experienced French traders. In England the charter afforded
the company no protection from competition with merchants
dealing in furs from New York, New England, or the Chesapeake, and on the European market it also had to compete
with the French importers and Dutch middlemen. In this
market climate, information became important to the
company's decision-making. Much knowledge was gleaned
from a network of people associated with the London fur
trade. Many of these informers are impossible to identify, but veiled references to information about the
competition in the minutes and letters outward connote
the importance of good contacts among London furriers, in
the customs house, in court, and in parliament.

---

[81]Minutes, 20 October 1681, in ibid., p. 134.

[82]Minutes, 9 December 1681, in ibid., p. 159.

[83]Minutes, 14 and 16 December 1681, in ibid., pp.
162, 164-65.

[84]Minutes, 5 January 1681/2, in ibid., p. 169.

[85]L.O. to Nixon, 15 May 1682, in Letters Outward,
vol. 11, p. 41.

On 28 October 1681 the committee decided to schedule
its next sale of beaver for Wednesday, 16 November.
Before the meeting ended Mr. Byfield, a furrier who
sorted the company's furs, arrived to say that a sale of
New York beaver had been scheduled for Tuesday, 15 November.   Thereupon the committee moved its sale ahead a
week to 9 November.[86] On the day of the sale the committee heard that a rumor was spreading that the arrival of
another of its ships from the bay was imminent. Fearing
that the furriers might wait out the company in hopes of
a larger supply and a better price, the committee decided
to declare "at the Candle [i.e., at the beginning of the
auction] that the Company doth not expect any other ship
this year and That They will not sell any other Goods
before Michaelmas next [September 29]."[87]

During the company's first two decades one of its
most important customers and informants was Thomas Glover, a large London furrier. How Glover received his news
is unclear.   In October 1690 he reported "from another"
that parliament had passed a law allowing the importation
of Dutch fur with a small duty. The committee met with
Glover to consider ways of blocking the act,[88] and also
asked the Solicitor General, Sir John Summers, to introd-
uce a bill to lay a duty on all imported beaver wool.[89]
On 12 November a Mr. Healer and a Mr. Baker, probably
furriers, approached the committee with the news that
beaver skins and wool were coming into England despite
the Navigation Acts and asked if the company would assume
part of the costs for a suit against the importers; the
committee agreed to pay two-thirds of the charge.[90]
Contacts in the customs house also kept the company
informed of movements of fur in and out of the port of

---

[86]Minutes, 28 October 1681, in Minutes, 1679-1684
vol. 8, pp. 137-38.

[87]Minutes, 9 November 1681, in ibid., p. 145. At
auctions during this period a candle was lit when the
upset price was given and bidding began. The highest
bidder when the candle sputtered out was the purchaser.
Rich, H.B.C., 1670-1870, vol. 1, p. 68.

[88]Minutes, 22 October 1690, Hudson's Bay Company
Archives, Provincial Archives of Manitoba (hereafter
HBCA, PAM), A.1/12, fo. 33d.

[89]Minutes, 25 October 1690, HBCA, PAM, A.1/12,
fo. 34d.

[90]Minutes, 12 November 1690, ibid., fo. 36.

London.   After impounding a shipment of Dutch beaver in
1692, the customs house sold the fur to the Hudson's Bay
Company for eight shillings a pound.[91]   The company paid
a high price in its efforts to restrict competitors on
the London market.   The average price per pound it received for beaver during this period was 6s.11d. in 1691,
8s.9d. in 1692, and 7 shillings in 1693.[92]   In two of the
years it would have lost money.   In 1692, when the average price was nine pence (or 11 percent) over the price
it paid for the Dutch furs, it would barely have covered
the costs of purchasing, transporting, and warehousing
the furs.

The company placed great value on maintaining good
relationships with London's furriers, as can be seen in
the conflict which arose over the 1690 sale of beaver to
Thomas Glover.   Wanting to purchase beaver, Glover approached the company in April 1690 to discuss what ar-
rangements could be made.[93]   A sub-committee agreed with
him to rig a sale in which coat beaver would be set up
at eleven shillings a pound, but would be sold at eight
shillings a pound to Glover who agreed to buy 100 lots at
that price.   At the committee meeting at which this ar-
rangement was disclosed Mr. Thomas Chambers, a member,
proposed a counter-offer of the same price plus two
hundred pounds.   "And it being debated in this Committee
whether they thought two hundred pounds advance a valuable Consideration for Rejecting the offer made by Mr.
Glover, it was put to the vote and by the Majority it
passed in the Negative."   After rejecting the offer of
Chambers, some committee members requested that the
Deputy Governor enjoin them "to an oath of secresey that
noe mention bee made out of the Committee Concerning the
agreement with Mr. Glover."[94]   On July 2 the sale was
held as planned, but Mr. Chambers and Mr. Foote, another
committee member, refused to participate.[95]   At the sale
a small retailer bought two hundred pieces of coat beaver

---

[91]Minutes, 2 November 1692; and Minutes, 25 November
1692, HBCA, PAM, A.1/14.

[92]Prices compiled from fur sales in the Grand
Journals, HBCA, PAM, A.15/3-A.15/5.

[93]Minutes, 15 April 1690, HBCA, PAM, A.1/12, fo. 14.

[94]Minutes, 25 June 1690, HBCA, PAM, A.1/12, fos. 23-
23d.

[95]Minutes, 2 July 1690, HBCA, PAM, A.1/12, fo. 24.

at 11s.2d. a pound, and Glover bought twenty thousand pieces at 8s.2d a pound.[96]

On 5 August 1690, at the General Court, the annual meeting of the company which all shareholders could attend and during which the officers and committee members were elected, Chambers submitted articles against the Deputy Governor and the rest of the committee for the handling of the 2 July sale. A great furor arose, the charges were denied, the accused committee members offered a vindication and proposed a discussion of the contested sale. A timely adjournment by the Governor, the Earl of Marlborough, due to the summer heat, tabled the whole matter and the shareholders were reminded to "Keepe Secrett the Debates and Transactions of this Generall Court."[97] The General Court convened again on 8 August and the committee came prepared to answer Chamber's charges and level its own against him. Chambers left. The General Court, in his absence, charged him with contempt and stripped him of his committee responsibilities and privileges.[98]

The company's internal conflict also had its external dimensions in the London and European fur market. Since 1688 the company had had difficulty disposing of its furs. Sixteen thousand coat beaver had remained unsold from the March 1688 sale. In November the company sold half of those furs, leaving 8000. At a December sale Mr. Skinner, a large London furrier, was the only purchaser of coat beaver and he bought only 800 skins. The company broached the possibility of a private sale to Skinner which resulted in a split in the General Court over whether to sell by public auction or private contract. The court ruled at its meeting in February 1689 that all sales would be by public auction by the candle unless it authorized the committee to negotiate private sales to dispose of excess furs. Having exerted its authority to dictate policy to the committee, the court immediately empowered the committee to dispose of the present stock of furs by private contract.[99] Transpiring simultaneously were challenges to the company's charter by the Company of Feltmakers of the City of London. The matter went to parliament in 1690, where the charter was

---

[96]Grand Ledger, HBCA, PAM, A.14/5, fo. 53.

[97]Minutes, 5 August 1690, HBCA, PAM, A.1/12, fol. 25.

[98]Rich, H.B.C., 1670-1870, vol. 1, p. 270.

[99]Ibid., pp. 258-59.

confirmed for another seven years, but with the added proviso that:

> the said Governor and Company shall make at least two public Sales of Coat Beaver in every year and not exceeding four and that they shall proportion the same into lots each of about one hundred pounds sterling but not exceeding two hundred pounds value. And that in the intervals of the public Sales the said Company may not sell Coat Beaver by private Contract at any lower price than it was set up at the last public Sale and that the Coat Beaver now in the Companies Hands shall be liable to the same rules.[100]

The proviso emphasized the marketing of coat beaver in order to pacify small retailers in the Company of Feltmakers who wanted access to it in quantities small enough to purchase directly from importers like the Hudson's Bay Company, and for the same price paid by large furriers. Parchment beaver did not interest them, for at this time the English lacked the knowledge to remove the long guard hairs, and so parchment beaver had to be sent to Russia for processing. The parliamentary proviso might have been adhered to had an excess of coat beaver not been coming into England, forcing the Hudson's Bay Company to treat with large furriers, like Thomas Glover, who exported much of what they bought. Two interrelated issues came into play: one, whether to sell large lots to exporters or small lots to retailers; and two, whether to sell by auction or private sale. Had the English market not been glutted it might have been possible to accommodate everyone, but the need to arrange suitable means of getting furs out of England encouraged the company to collude with exporters of furs, and added to the conflict within the company.

For the years prior to 1694 it is impossible to judge how many of the furs from Hudson Bay were re-exported, but in 1694 the company began sending its own consignments of furs to agents in Amsterdam, Hamburg, and Narva, Estonia. Between 1694 and 1698 it exported 58,965 parchment beaver skins and 40,166 coat beaver skins[101] out of the total sales of 90,902 parchment beaver and

---

[100]Ibid., p. 269.

[101]Journal of Foreign Accounting, 1694-1706, HBCA, PAM, A.17/2, fo. 42.

60,486 coat beaver,[102] or sixty-five percent of total
sales.   Of the 45,466 pelts shipped to Amsterdam 5,250
were re-exported to Archangel, Russia; of the 49,203
pelts shipped to Hamburg 7,200 were re-exported to Narva
and 32,292 to Archangel.[103] Agents in Narva and Archangel then exchanged furs for Baltic products, among them
hog bristles, flax, goat skins, hides, hemp, jute,
tallow, and beaver wool which the company then had to
sell in western Europe.[104] The returns from this trade
came very slowly.   In 1701 the company's agent in
Amsterdam finally disposed of 8,500 coat beaver skins at
4s.8d. a pound, much less than the price of six shillings
a pound, the value at which they were first entered in
the account books.[105]   In 1701 and 1707 the company
consigned furs to committeeman John Nicholson for export
to Russia; the returns from these furs again came slowly
and were only generated through the importation of
Russian hemp, some of which arrived as late as 1711.[106]

The direct involvement of the Hudson's Bay Company
with re-exporting beaver pelts reveals a few important
features of the fur market within which it operated.
The first and most obvious feature was the glutted
English market for furs and the need to dispose of some
of those furs elsewhere.   The second was that direct
participation in the intra-European trade demanded a
commitment to a longer turn-around time after an initial
investment and an ability and willingness of the company
to carry that cost.   The time lengthened considerably
when the Hudson's Bay Company had to sell Russian commodities in order to finalize transactions.   Third, the
company had to compete with well established middlemen,
such as Glover.

Assessing the gains from this trade, especially the
exchange of North American furs for Russian products, is
virtually impossible. Between 1694 and 1706 the company
kept a Journal of Foreign Accounting. The final profit

---

[102]Compiled from Grand Journals, HBCA, PAM, A.15/3-5.

[103]Journal of Foreign Accounting, HBCA, PAM, A.17/2,
fos. 1, 5, 17-20, 39, 58, 87, 101.

[104]Ibid., fos. 36-39, 42, 59, 70.

[105]Ibid., fo. 138.

[106]Minutes, HBCA, PAM, A.1/23. fos. 27d-28; Grand
Journals, HBCA, PAM, A.15/5, fos. 74-78, 142-43; and E.
E. Rich, H.B.C., 1670-1870, vol. 1, p. 461.

and loss balance lists a gain of £7856.9s.5d. on furs calculated at a value of £35,508.14s.[107] This amounted to a gain of twenty-two percent, yet it was spread over a twelve year period on furs shipped from 1694 to 1698. The Journal of Foreign Accounting includes no expenses for procuring the furs, nor for the interest charges on the money the company borrowed during this period, costs which were carried instead in the Grand Ledger. Therefore, the actual gains were much lower. However, by exporting furs itself, the company may have been avoiding some of the need to collude with the large furriers such as Thomas Glover, whose privileged buying position had caused conflict within the company, with parliament and with the Company of Feltmakers. Re-exporting may have also given the company marginally more market control. Regardless of possible advantages, however, the process was too involved for the company to continue the practice if avoidable.

From the records of both the customs house and the company it is possible to gain some appreciation of the magnitude of the increased volume of beaver coming into England from North America after 1697, the first year for which customs records are extant. Table 1 presents the customs house totals for all of British North America including New England, Pennsylvania, Maryland and Virginia, the volume imported from Hudson Bay, the company's percentage of the total, and the combined percentage of the New York and Hudson Bay trade. In the far right column of table 1 are the figures taken from the company's records. These figures are consistently higher than the customs house figures. To evade paying all the customs fees the company instructed the men at the forts to pack heavy furs forty to forty-five to a bundle and thin furs fifty-five to sixty to a bundle. This practice would have tended to make all bundles nearly the same size. The thin light furs were then to be stowed on the ship first so that they came off last,[108] after the customs valuation had been done. The ploy must have worked. Thus the glut of beaver on the English market was even greater than the customs records tell.[109]

---

[107] Journal of Foreign Accounting, HBCA, PAM, A.17/2, fos. 41-42.

[108] L.O. to Fullartine, 26 May 1708, HBCA, PAM, A.6/3, fo. 90d.

[109] McCusker and Menard in The Economy of British America say that for scholars using the customs records "smuggling was less of a problem than might be imagined" (p. 77). This may be true for other colonial commodities, but it is a problem for scholars of the fur trade.

34

Table 1: English Beaver Imports, 1697-1726

Year	Customs Total	HBC per Customs	HBC % Total	HBC & NY % Total	Co.	HBC per Records
1697	42,902	34,341	80%	83%		42,990
1698	3,165	60	2%	2%		0
1699	54,508	20,477	38%	79%		33,741
1700	39,989	12,669	32%	73%		19,329
1701	22,536	30	0%	50%		0
1702	20,501	9,244	45%	58%		14,838
1703	35,356	30,089	85%	92%		42,080
1704	12,851	---	0%	28%		0
1705	0	---	0%	0%		0
1706	38,294	33,212	87%	87%		50,092
1707	6,474	---	0%	45%		25,943
1708	38,477	14,680	38%	63%		12,680
1709	34,665	7,344	21%	68%		0
1710	8,987	---	0%	60%		0
1711	23,438	2,000	9%	38%		51,129
1712	0	---	0%	0%		51,025
1713	63,515	36,663	58%	84%		0
1714	86,127	34,909	41%	78%		42,848
1715	28,969	---	0%	39%		0
1716	92,364	65,931	71%	91%		76,718
1717	73,709	41,475	56%	83%		55,554
1718	80,990	41,186	51%	88%		48,177
1719	43,646	18,606	43%	84%		20,694
1720	83,600	52,594	63%	95%		55,483
1721	78,670	52,231	66%	96%		60,899
1722	86,645	58,368	67%	97%		65,434
1723	80,117	56,693	71%	99%		63,222
1724	56,052	32,565	58%	100%		36,731
1725	92,337	57,808	63%	97%		60,855
1726	88,956	48,593	55%	96%		52,364

Table 2: HBC & NY Share of Beaver Imports, 1697-1727

Five-Year Averages	HBC	NY	Combined
1697-1701	41%	32%	73%
1702-1706	68%	8%	76%
1707-1711	21%	37%	58%
1712-1716	51%	29%	80%
1717-1721	57%	33%	90%
1722-1727	63%	35%	98%

Sources: Customs Records, collected by Arthur J. Ray
Grand Journals, HBCA, PAM, A.15/2-A.15/8.

The increased volume of beaver from Hudson Bay alone would have forced adjustments in the English fur market. The almost simultaneous growth of the Hudson Bay trade and the New York trade dramatically reshaped the market (table 2). While the customs house figures are surely low and do not date from the beginning of the company they do help to explain why the Hudson's Bay Company was forced into colluding with exporters or exporting furs itself to relieve the glut of beaver in England. They also suggest why the price for beaver dropped so precipitously in the 1690s.

The average prices at which the Hudson's Bay Company sold fur from 1682 to 1726 are listed in Table 3. The figures represent an average price per piece rather than an average price per pound which is the way the company sold beaver. The prices are calculated in this way largely to facilitate the later discussion of the trade with the Indians from whom the company originally purchased the fur on a per piece basis. Stating the price by the piece rather than by the pound gives a better picture of the difference in value between a coat beaver and a parchment beaver pelt. For example, coat beaver sold at 7s.10d. per pound in 1692 which was an average of 8s.2d. per piece. A year later parchment sold for 7s.5d. per pound, but the average value was 8s.11d. per piece. A coat beaver pelt, deriving its name from its prior use in Indian coats, weighed approximately thirty percent less than a parchment skin (which had never been used for clothing) due to loss of the long guard hairs and loss to trimming and stitching.[110]

---

[110]From 1684 to 1699 the average weight of coat beaver was 1.06 lbs. per pelt (0.98 lb. to 1.15 lb. range) and parchment an average of 1.30 lbs. (1.15 lb. to 1.53 lb. range). Calculated from fur sale records, Grand Journals and Grand Ledgers. Harold A. Innis in The Fur Trade in Canada: An Introduction to Canadian Economic History, rev. ed. (Toronto: Univ. of Toronto Press, 1970), p. 4, describes a beaver pelt as weighing from 1.5 to 1.75 pounds. Innis' range is much higher than that for the pelts coming out of Hudson Bay in the seventeenth century. Murray Lawson in Fur, a Study in English Mercantilism, 1700-1775, (Toronto: Univ. of Toronto Press, 1943), p. 136, estimates the number of beaver exports from Canada in the eighteenth century using Innis' lower range of one and a half pounds as a conversion. It is probable that his figures are fifteen to thirty-three percent too low.

36

Table 3: Average Price per Piece of Beaver, 1682-1726

Year	Coat	Parchment	Wgt'd. Avg.
1682	14 : 2	12 : 3	13 : 1
1683	9 : 3	11 :11	9 :10
1684	8 : 7	13 : 7	10 : 8
1685	8 : 4	11 :10	10 : 4
1686	10 : 1	12 : 1	10 :11
1687	12 : 1	10 : 3	11 : 0
1688	11 : 1	13 :11	12 : 7
1689	8 : 8	13 : 3	10 : 7
1690	- : -	10 : 0	10 : 0
1691	6 : 4	8 :11	8 : 6
1692	8 : 2	11 : 5	10 : 3
1693	7 : 1	8 :11	8 : 0
1694	7 : 8	10 : 1	9 : 1
1695	8 : 1	10 : 7	9 : 7
1696	8 : 0	10 : 1	9 : 8
1697	6 : 2	7 : 9	7 : 1
1698	5 : 7	10 :10	7 :11
1699	4 : 1	6 : 6	5 : 1
1700	4 : 7	6 : 5	6 : 1
1701	3 :10 *	- : -	3 :10 *
1702	5 : 5	9 : 1	6 : 4
1703	5 : 4	- : -	5 : 4
1704	- : -	5 : 9	5 : 9
1705	- : -	- : -	- : -
1706	5 : 1	- : -	5 : 1
1707	- : -	6 : 9	6 : 9
1708	5 : 5	6 :10	6 : 2
1709	- : -	5 :11	5 :11
1710	? : ?	? : ?	? : ?
1711	? : ?	? : ?	? : ?
1712	? : ?	? : ?	? : ?
1713	4 : 8	5 :11	5 : 4
1714	7 :11	5 : 2	5 : 6
1715	- :-	- : -	- : -
1716	8 : 5	4 : 8	5 : 0
1717	8 : 4	5 : 2	5 :10
1718	7 : 4	4 :11	5 : 1
1719	6 : 6	4 : 7	5 : 3
1720	5 :10	5 : 7	5 : 8
1721	5 :10	5 : 0	5 : 2
1722	5 : 0	4 : 7	4 : 9
1723	5 : 7	6 : 5	6 : 3
1724	6 : 0	6 : 7	6 : 5
1725	6 : 4	5 :10	5 :11
1726	7 : 5	5 : 0	5 : 8

* old coat beaver only
? no known sales
- no sales
: shillings:pence

Sources: Grand Journals, HBCA, PAM, A.15/1-15/8 and
         Grand Ledgers, A.14/2-A.14/9.

Table 3 shows that the price of beaver declined dramatically after 1696 and stabilized in the first quarter of the eighteenth century at approximately one-half of the prices in the 1680s. (In the 1730s prices would begin to rise again following the trend of the larger economy of England.) The figures suggest that to maintain a market for the large volume of furs coming in, the price had to remain relatively low. Even so, the Hudson's Bay Company began distributing annual dividends in 1718, indicating that it had recovered financially. Clearly, the company must have made significant adjustments in its overall operations in order to counteract this major price transition in the European fur market.

The direct influence the Hudson's Bay Company had on the market prices of fur was through control of the volume of furs it brought to the market. As noted previously, market information played a crucial role in the company's decisions about how many furs to put on the auction block, or whether to dispose of furs on foreign markets. Marketing strategy acquired growing importance in the operation of the company. It necessitated recognizing and determining the profitable limits of the market and then operating within those parameters. In turn, this recognition placed constraints on the extent to which trade could expand before those limits were met. During the 1670s, 1680s, and 1690s the beaver trade expanded beyond English and continental market demand. In the first decades of the eighteenth century, the market became capable of carrying a larger volume of furs but at the cost of lower prices. Therefore, to survive financially in the fur trade the Hudson's Bay Company had to adapt its operations to the new market parameters which its own advent had helped to reshape. Regulating the flow of furs coming onto the market was one strategy it employed.

To control the volume of furs in Europe the Hudson's Bay Company had to monitor the flow from North America in order to avoid excessive stockpiles in London warehouses. Modest stockpiles in London were desirable as insurance against miscarriage or delay in shipments from the bay, to respond to moderate fluctuations in market demand, or to take up market slack should a competitor be caught with inadequate supplies. Large stockpiles, however, tied up working capital and depressed the market. In the 1690s, when coat beaver was accumulating in the company's London warehouses, the committee instructed the traders at the bay to discourage the Indians from bringing in coat beaver.[111]   Upon orders from London Governor Fullartine shipped no coat or stage beaver[112] in 1708, leaving it to accumulate in the Albany warehouse.[113] This had two effects: it delayed the customs expenses in London, and it reduced the beaver available on the London market without having to turn away Indian traders in North America. Two years later, the London stockpiles of coat beaver had been reduced and the men at the bay were told to ship 12,000 of the best coat beaver to London.[114] By 1713 and the Treaty of Utrecht, stockpiles in England had been nearly eliminated due largely to reduced imports; only 14,488 parchment beaver and 8,636 coat beaver remained in the company's London warehouse.[115]

Table 4 shows the volume of imports, the volume of sales and estimates of the furs remaining in the London warehouse. The figures indicate the strategy of controlling volume which the management of the Hudson's Bay Company evolved after the glut in the 1690s. As exact values these figures, especially those in the warehouse column, should be used cautiously. This column begins with the assumption of a zero value for 1680 since data for the first decade are very spotty. Consequently there are some negative values in column 3, suggesting that the company very probably had some fur backlogs in the 1680s. As well, the Dutch furs purchased from the customs house in 1692 are not included in the imports and further skew the warehouse figures. Therefore, until 1712 the warehouse figures are to illustrate the relationship between imports and sales. In 1713, before the fall sale, the company took an inventory of beaver pelts in order to balance its ledger, and the warehouse figures after that time are quite accurate. That inventory figure is listed in the 1712 row because it predated the 1713 fur sales. The import volumes are taken from the journal valuations which the company began in 1684, retroactive to 1681, and are accurate, save for the Dutch furs purchased in 1692.

---

[111]L.O. to Governor Geyer, 22 May 1690, Letters Outward, vol. 20, p. 98.

[112]Stage (cf French, étiage) pelts are from animals trapped in the summer when the fur is thinner.

[113]L.O. to Governor Fullartine, 26 May 1708, HBCA, PAM, A.6/3, fos. 90d-91.

[114]L.O. to Governor Fullartine, 29 May 1710, HBCA, PAM, A.6/3, fo. 101.

[115]Grand Journal, HBCA, PAM, A.15/6, fo. 1.

Table 4: Import, Sales, and Warehouse Volumes

Year	Imports	Sales	W'house
1681	24,123	25,062	(939)
1682	18,690	8,956	8,795
1683	20,075	25,034	3,836
1684	18,924	17,345	5,415
1685	14,950	16,972	3,393
1686	20,152	19,955	3,590
1687	20,485	18,491	5,584
1688	20,928	22,200	4,312
1689	27,201	34,727	(3,214)
1690	37,520	12,373	21,933
1691	28,117	29,388	20,662
1692	24,236	33,223	11,675
1693	92,349	34,989	69,035
1694	62,005	55,983	75,057
1695	0	32,668	42,389
1696	19,623	20,002	42,010
1697	42,990	42,841	42,159
1698	0	13,130	29,029
1699	33,741	30,616	32,154
1700	19,329	15,610	35,873
1701	0	40,000	(4,127)
1702	14,838	24,128	(13,417)
1703	42,080	9,994	18,669
1704	0	21,720	(3,051)
1705	0	0	(3,051)
1706	50,092	7,500	39,541
1707	25,943	22,536	42,948
1708	12,680	16,084	39,544
1709	0	1,680	37,864
1710	0	?	?
1711	51,129	?	?
1712	51,025	?	23,124*
1713	0	20,271	2,853
1714	42,848	37,549	8,152
1715	0	0	8,152
1716	76,718	70,211	14,659
1717	55,554	52,795	17,418
1718	48,177	45,900	19,695
1719	20,694	27,905	12,484
1720	55,483	39,366	28,601
1721	60,899	59,754	29,746
1722	65,434	71,614	23,566
1723	63,222	64,885	21,903
1724	36,731	40,432	18,202
1725	60,855	62,606	16,451
1726	52,364	53,656	15,159

* from the Grand Ledger, 30 Sept before the 1713 sales

? sales unknown

Sources: Grand Journals, HBCA, PAM, A.15/1-15/8 and
         Grand Ledgers, A.14/2-A.14/9

Despite these problems, the overall configuration of the figures sketches a relatively accurate picture of the turnover of the inventory. Throughout the 1680s imports and sales moved in tandem. Then in 1690 sales slumped, imports jumped, and the company's fur surplus grew. With the capture of York Fort from the French in 1693 and the acquisition of their furs, stockpiles climbed to 70,000 pelts, a two to three year backlog. The inability of the company to dispose of its inventory probably crippled it as much as did the decline in prices. Excess inventory not only glutted the market but also represented production costs which could not be recovered easily. To reduce its inventory, the company exported furs to continental Europe and reduced its imports from the bay. In six of the fourteen years from 1700 to 1713 the company received no shipments from the bay. In some of those years the company chose not to send out a ship for "the badness of the Markett for Beaver would not Answer our Charge."[116] In other years the hazards of wartime shipping and the difficulty of getting seamen precluded voyages to Hudson Bay.[117]

The peacetime years after 1713 allowed the company to regulate its affairs much more closely. The inventory it carried over from year to year never exceeded sales. The committee learned not to eliminate stockpiles completely. In 1715 no ship returned from the bay and the letters outward the following year contain complaints of the hardship caused in London.[118] In 1719 a decline in volume of furs imported also created a one-year decline in sales even though the company had another 11,000 furs in its warehouse. The pattern for other years is very similar with volume of imports and sales very close and a modest stockpile retained in the warehouse.

In long-distance trade during the early modern period, investments in inventories to cover a year's sale in the event of shipping difficulties became an important mechanism for mitigating market uncertainty, creating greater market control, and thereby granting greater long-term financial security. Stockpiles of beaver were maintained in London, and trade goods were stockpiled at

[116]L.O. to Governor Fullartine, 1701, HBCA, PAM, A.6/3, fo. 47.

[117]L.O. to Governor Fullartine, 3 June 1702, HBCA, PAM, A.6/3, fos. 52-52d.

[118]L.O. to Governor Knight, 15 May 1715, HBCA, PAM, A.6/4, fo. 3.

the bay posts. This involved large investments, both in working capital for inventories and fixed capital for warehouses. It also necessitated a sophisticated managerial and administrative structure to oversee the operation. This conservative approach to trade was directed towards the goal of long-term survival rather than short-term profits. Much credit for the financial recovery of the Hudson's Bay Company after the glutted market of the 1690s and the decline in beaver prices must be given to the management of the beaver market which the company evolved. Attention to market information and control of inventories were very important factors.

The control of inventories rested on one particular advantage possessed by the Hudson's Bay Company. Since it did not have to contend with permanent settlers pressing their own trading interests in this period, it had greater flexibility to monitor the volume of trade in North America in relationship to the volume of sales in Europe. This is perhaps a crucial difference between the Hudson's Bay Company and the Canadian fur trade, or the English fur trade in New York. In the century before the British conquest of New France, the Canadians shipped many more furs to France than the Hudson's Bay Company did to England. Superficially this suggests that the French were more successful than the English, but this would only be true from a commercial perspective if trade in North America did not outpace sales in Europe. If it did, then it would prove commercially disastrous. If the French beaver trade was commercially bankrupt after the 1690s, the cause may have been its over-production of furs rather than the decline in prices. It is telling that when the Hudson's Bay Company had excess profits to invest in the 1720s and 1730s it did not expand the fur trade, but invested instead in South Sea Company annuities and East India Company bonds.[119] The continued desire to diversify trade and investments and lessen the dependence on beaver indicates that the Hudson's Bay Company had discovered the limits of the beaver trade and chose not to move beyond them. The ability of the Hudson's Bay Company to adapt its trade to the European fur market through attention to market information and control of inventories figures significantly in any assessment of its financial recovery after the 1690s and of its long-term survival. This qualifies emphasis given to trade volume or price, neither of which offers a sufficient explanation of who survived in the fur trade and why they did so.

---

[119]Grand Ledger, HBCA, PAM, A.14/8, fos. 32, 100; and Grand Journal, A.15/7, fo. 150.

Chapter 3

TRADE GOODS MANAGEMENT

The two greatest management and administrative tasks for the committee in London entailed preparation for the spring dispatch of the company's ships and organization of the fur sales after the autumn return. The fortunes of the company rested on the sound management of these two spheres of activity. The timing of sales, the volume of furs offered, the volume of furs imported, and the activities of competitors demanded careful attention. Similar care had to be taken with the purchase of trade goods. A myriad of details concerning the quality, quantity, price, selection, and supply of merchandise occupied much of the committee's time from January to May. Coordinating trade goods purchases in England with the demands of Canadian subarctic Indians posed both financial and organizational difficulties, and in the early years the company's methods for procuring trade goods and controlling inventory were often haphazard, experimental, and consequently costly. Problems of insufficiency, such as occurred in 1681, could be remedied only too easily by creating problems of excess. Thus procedures had to be devised to assure adequate supplies and to avoid insufficient or excessive supplies. In addition, the drop in fur prices in the 1690s compelled the company to rationalize further all aspects of its business, and efficient management of the trading inventory absorbed some of the financial shock of the price transition in the European fur market. Slowly, the company developed systematic procedures for purchasing merchandise and controlling the size of the trade inventory, which, by the second decade of the eighteenth century, assured relative cost efficiency in this part of its business.

One of the first problems with which the company had to grapple was simply what to buy. The wisdom of hindsight and long practice makes the choices seem simple: guns and related accessories, knives, hatchets, kettles, blankets, Brazil tobacco, brandy, and beads. These few stock items of the trade, however, became standard after many years of experience on the part of both the company and the Indians; blankets, Brazil tobacco, and brandy were later additions to the inventory. Many other items the company purchased only once or twice, and when they had been traded or had rusted or rotted beyond repair they were not replaced. Lack of knowledge about what the Indians wanted occasioned wide latitude for errors of judgement.

The cargo for 1670, the year of the company's charter, included beads, looking-glasses, combs, guns and accessories, hatchets, kettles, knives, arrowheads, and duffel.[120] Alert to the possibilities of improving its trading position, the Hudson's Bay Company gradually introduced new goods which became stock items of its trade. Its Grand Ledger from November 1681 to November 1684 included "The Acct. of Samples," and listed purchases of kettles, chisels, hawk bells, scrapers, hatchets, blankets, and guns.[121] Blankets slowly gained prominence. For the 1678 cargo the committee bought a total of six pieces of kersey blanketting from three different people, probably as trial purchases.[122] By 1682 the company was purchasing a much larger number of blankets, many from Oxfordshire.[123] That same year the committee arranged to have samples of French blankets sent to it.[124] They arrived but the response to them is unclear, though the 1684 shipment to Fort Albany included ten French blankets in addition to 350 others.[125] Until 1685 the company only traded Virginia tobacco, but that

---

[120]E. E. Rich, intro., Minutes of the Hudson's Bay Company, 1671-1674 (London: Hudson's Bay Record Society, vol. 5, 1942), p. xxxi.

[121]Grand Ledger, HBCA, PAM, A.14/4, fo. 97d.

[122]Grand Journal, HBCA, PAM, A.15/1, fos. 8-8d, 10.

[123]Minutes, 3 March 1681/2, in Minutes of the Hudson's Bay Company, 1679-1684, ed. E. E. Rich (London: Hudson's Bay Record Society, vol. 8, 1945) p. 189. See Grand Journal, HBCA, PAM, A.15/2, fos. 31, 33 for 1682 blanket purchases. Individual blankets were cut from large pieces of cloth. As blankets became a regular item of trade, it became standard that one piece of cloth would contain enough fabric for about fifteen blankets. See Invoice Books, HBCA, PAM, A.24/2, fo. 20d (1710) and A.24/2, fo. 43d (1714).

[124]Minutes, 25 January 1681/2, Rich, p. 177, and Grand Journal, HBCA, PAM, A.15/2, fo. 41d.

[125]Invoice Books, HBCA, PAM, A.24/1, fos. 3-3d.

year it adopted the French practice of importing Brazil tobacco, the variety preferred by the Indians, from the Portuguese.[126]   Thereafter the company went to great lengths to obtain this South American luxury. In 1708 and again in 1715 supplies from Portugal were disrupted, causing the company to purchase it at markedly higher prices through merchants in the Netherlands.[127] In 1718 Brazil tobacco was not available at all, and in 1724 the order from Portugal did not arrive in time to make the spring dispatch of the company's ships.[128]   Brandy, another staple of the trade, was first listed as a trade good in the Albany Fort account books of 1698, and at York Fort in 1718.[129] After the Treaty of Utrecht in 1713 rundlets or kegs in one, two and three gallon sizes were one of the few new items introduced.[130]

Being remote from Hudson Bay, the committee depended greatly on the advice of traders when ordering trade goods, especially in the early years. After returning from service at the bay, traders often attended committee meetings and the early minutes and annual letters frequently mention their assistance:

"Mr. Bailey gives his opinion accordeing to an

---

[126]L.O. to Sergeant, 22 May 1685 in Letters Outward, 1679-1694, ed. E. E. Rich (London: Hudson's Bay Record Society, vol. 11, 1948) p. 142.

[127]Letter to Nicolas Spilman, Amsterdam, 1708, HBCA, PAM, A.6/3, fos. 88-89; and L.O. to Knight at York Fort, 3 June 1715, A.6/3, fo. 133d. In 1705 the company paid eleven pence for Brazil tobacco and in 1708 paid 2s.1d., an increase of 127.5 percent in price.

[128]L.O. to McCliesh, 30 May 1718, HBCA, PAM, A.6/4, fo. 22d; and L.O. to McCliesh, 1724, A.6/4, fo. 85d.

[129]Albany Fort Account Book, 1698-99, HBCA, PAM, B.3/9, fos. 41d-42; and York Fort Account Books, 1718-19, HBCA, PAM, B.239/d/10, fo. 6d.

[130]Albany Fort Account Book, 1718-19, HBCA, PAM, B.3/d/27, fo. 7; and York Fort Account Book, 1721-22, B.239/d/12, fo. 32d. Arthur J. Ray has suggested that rundlets possibly allowed the Indians to transport the brandy inland (personal communication). There was a rise in the percentage of brandy traded as a percentage of the total trade after the introduction of kegs at Fort Albany, but it is not clear that the cause of the rise was the availability of carrying vessels.

order formerly made that for an additionnal cargo for the year ensueing there may bee Suplyed ..." (1671/2)[131]

"Wee have taken the advise of Mr. Knight and Mr. Bridgar, whome wee have found very ingenious and knowing men in the business of our trade." (1682)[132]

"We have sent you by Mr. Knights Directions 100 party Cullerd coates ..." (1684)[133]

"Mr. Piere Radison haveing viewed over the Merchantdeis cargo and does judge that 500 Ice Chissells be added more." (1685)[134]

Despite sagacious advice from experienced traders, a considerable degree of guesswork persisted in the selection of merchandise through the end of the seventeenth century.[135] In the 1690s the company offered the Indians an array of cloth to rival that offered by an English shopkeeper: silk, serge, Scottish plaids, shalloon, canvas duck, perpetuanas, broadcloth, duffel, baize, cotton, flannel, and blankets.[136] By 1713 and the repossession of York Fort, the company had learned that it only paid to stock broadcloth, duffel, blankets, and small quantities of baize and flannel.[137] During the 1680s and 1690s the forts housed a virtual clothier's shop in an attempt to coax the Indians out of their fur garments; coats, shirts, pants, hats, caps, socks, shoes,

---

[131]Minutes, 16 January 1671/2, Minutes, 1671-1674, vol. 5, p. 19.

[132]L.O. to Nixon, 15 May 1682, Letters Outward, vol. 11, p. 38.

[133]L.O. to Sergeant, 16 May 1684, ibid., p. 126.

[134]Minutes, 1 April 1685, HBCA, PAM, A.1/8, fo. 23.

[135]Minutes, HBCA, PAM, A.1/8, fos. 4d, 6d, 8d, 17d, 19d, 23, 25, 28.

[136]York Fort Account Books, HBCA, PAM, B.239/d/3, fos. 10d-11; B.239/d/4, fos. 9d-10; and Albany Fort Account Book, HBCA, PAM, B.3/d/2, fos. 29-62.

[137]Compare the 1693-94 York Fort Account Book, HBCA, PAM, B.239/d/5, fos. 18-18d, with a post-Treaty of Utrecht account book such as B.239/d/11, fos. 2d-3.

mittens, gloves, sashes, handkerchiefs, and women's sleeves in assorted sizes and varieties were stocked.[138] By the early eighteenth century handkerchiefs and women's sleeves had disappeared from the selection; coats and pants became trade gifts; and the variety of other items was reduced considerably. The committee purchased curiosities and trinkets with which to tempt the Indians: arm, neck, and nose jewels, ivory and copper pipes, travelling spectacles, jews'-harps, cat-calls, and whistles.[139] But the subarctic Indians desired only a limited number of trinkets, chiefly beads, feathers, looking-glasses, and rings. The Indians readily traded for most metal goods, but rejected the company's offer of metal arrowheads, which rusted on the shelf and were finally discarded.[140]

The range of trial goods which passed through the company's warehouses illustrates the experimental character of its early purchases. Many of these goods were investments which the company recovered slowly, if at all. No silk, arrowheads, black hats, or waistcoats were traded at York Fort from July 1690 to July 1691. Only one of 322 women's sleeves, and five of 399 jewels attracted any trade. The pattern is roughly the same in the following years. Nor were these goods popular as gifts.[141] The experimentation with many goods also indicates how long it took the company (nearly four decades) to determine the range of goods it paid to stock.

Controlling the volume of inventory was probably the most important aspect of trade goods management. Inadequate inventories discouraged the Indians from coming to trade; excessive inventories were costly. Merchants in the seventeenth and eighteenth centuries, like merchants today, wanted to recover their investment in inventory as quickly as possible, and tried to avoid tying up working capital in dead or slow-moving stock. Yet, as the Hudson's Bay Company learned, long-distance trade necessit-

---

[138]York Fort Account Books, HBCA, PAM, B.239/d/1, fos. 53-53d, B.239/d/4, fo. 21d; and Albany Fort Account Book, HBCA, PAM, B.3/d/2, fos. 29-62.

[139]York Fort Account Book, HBCA, PAM, B.239/d/3, fos. 15d-39, and Albany Fort Account Book, HBCA, PAM, B.3/d/7, fo. 16.

[140]Albany Fort Account Books, HBCA, PAM, B.3/d/2, fos. 29-62; and B.3/d/7, fo. 16.

[141]York Fort Account Book, HBCA, PAM, B.239/d/3, fos. 15d-37.

ated a two-year supply of goods as insurance against the miscarriage of a cargo and, consequently, larger warehouse capacity for storage. The investment for inventory -- merchandise and warehouses -- was greater in long-distance trade as a percentage of the annual business than in many other areas of commerce, a cost which shareholders had to be willing to bear. Large inventories stocked over longer periods of time increased the chances for damage and deterioration. The committee in London occasionally saw fit to remind the men at the bay to take precautions to prevent the rusting of iron goods,[142] and to turn the barrels of gunpowder.[143] And the stock had to be rotated, old being traded before new. But still there was stock which ended up being thrown out. In 1693 the company re-established itself at Albany and had York Fort send extra trade goods from its stock. Upon receiving the merchandise, the Albany Fort traders complained that their York Fort counterparts had "laid hold of the opportunity to Clear their Warehouse of all their Lumbering Rubbish."[144] Three years later the Albany governor threw out many of those goods along with other untradeable merchandise.[145]

Time lags complicated the management of the inventory, for the committee in London had to plan twelve to eighteen months ahead of the operations at the bay. It gradually came to rely on annual correspondence, indents from the traders, and the account books from the forts to coordinate purchases in England with the trading needs in North America. It is doubtful whether the company originally realized the necessity for this careful record-keeping and a well structured administrative system. The early minutes contain no analysis of the fort records as do the later minutes and letters outward. Starting in the 1680s the letters outward stressed the

[142]L.O. to Sergeant, 16 May 1684, Letters Outward, vol. 11, p. 125.

[143]L.O. to Geyer, 6 June 1689, Letters Outward, 1688-1696, ed. E. E. Rich (London: Hudson's Bay Record Society, vol. 20, 1957), p. 61.

[144]Albany Fort Account Book, 1693-94, HBCA, PAM, B.3/d/2, fo. 1d.

[145]Albany Fort Account Book, 1695-1696, HBCA, PAM, B.3/d/7, fo. 16.

prove bookkeeping at a very basic level.[146]   In London
very rudimentary accounting methods were used until the
early 1680s and it is unlikely that more elaborate accounting would have been employed at the bay.   Only at
the end of the 1670s, with the transition in shareholders
from men of the Court to men of the City, was a simple
form of double-entry accounting introduced.[147]   Careful
accounting of the trade in North America probably began
at the same time, and with it came greater attempts to
synchronize the two arenas of the company's business.

In the correspondence from Hudson Bay to London the
chief trader would usually include an indent or order for
trade goods.   As the committee began to have trading
records to analyze, it also started to scrutinize indents
from the bay.   Finding Henry Sergeant's 1683 order far in
excess of the volume of trade he transacted, the committee elaborated upon its superabundance in the following
spring's annual letter.

"The Invoice of Goods you say that is wanting in
the Countrey we Judge is very Extravagant for your
Advicer has done it without consideration as in
some things we will touch upon to make you sensible
of the rest.

         You wold have 350 short guns of 3 1/2
foote   for HI 100 ditto 4 & 4 1/2...
Mr. Knight he writes for 700 guns of all seizes
                   1150 in all

Now consider what quantety you sell in a yeare
              at RR[148]   13
              at HI   26
              at AR   324
                         363 in all

And by your Accte. there are 962 remaineing in the
Countrey (though our bookes mentions 991) yet take
your Accte. thereof there are enough to last you

---

   [146]L.O. to Nixon, 15 May 1682; and L.O. to Sergeant,
16 May 1684 in Letters Outward, vol. 11, pp. 45, 48, 120,
122-24.

   [147]Compare the Grand Ledgers 1667-75 and 1676-82,
HBCA, PAM, A.14/1 and A.14/3.

   [148]RR: Rupert River at the southeast end of the bay;
HI: Hayes Island on the Moose River, an early site of
Moose Fort; AR: Albany River, the site of Albany Fort.

your Accte. thereof there are enough to last you above 2 yeares and a halfes Trade & now we are upon this subject we would have you remove our Merchantdizes & likewise Provissions which does exceed two years supply from one Factorey to the other where is most need as at RR 118 guns & sell by 13 in a yeare at HI 414 & sell but 26 in a yeare at both which places they Ley & rust to our Detriment & remove them to Albany River where our Chiefe Trad is only leaveing 2 yeares supplie of such guns as do most usually sell and so for shott you have remaining 39945 li. by your accte. (though ours mention 45047 li.) and you sell at

AR	8250	li.
HI	485	
RR	1000	
	9735	li. in a yeare

which remainder of shott is sufficient for 4 yeares Trade by your owne computation and yet you write for HI 19600 li. [lb] & sell but 485 li. in a yeare & there you have remaineing li. 13675 Mr. Knight writes for 21500 li. and he sells but 8250 li. and there is remaineing at his factorey 26386 li. by both which examples we think may convince you of such extravigant Demands and so many other sortes of goods our Rules have beene & shall be to supply you with all sortes of Merchantdizes for 2 yeares yet we have in some goods exceeded those Rules this yeare as in gun shott & powder etc.[149]

Much of the confusion resulted from the failure to account precisely for the disposal of all the company's goods, not just those traded but also goods expended for other purposes. A sizeable part of the stock of guns, shot, and powder was used by the men in hunting. For example, in 1721-22 the men at Albany Fort expended 337 pounds of gunpowder, 1360 pounds of shot, and 332 flints among assorted other goods.[150] The trading stock provided payments to the Indians for miscellaneous services, and gifts to them also reduced the inventory. Some goods, such as shot and guns, came in several varieties and had to be inventoried separately, which did not always happen. "[L]ikewise acquaint the Bookkeeper that for the future he mention in the Book of Accts the parti-

---

[149]L.O. to Sergeant, 16 May 1684, Letters Outward, vol. 11, pp. 122-24.

[150]Albany Fort Account Book, 1721-22, HBCA, PAM, B.3/d/30, fo. 11.

cular Number & Sorts of Guns traded, as likewise particularly by the Sorts of Shott."[151] Kettles were sold by
the pound, but only slowly did the committee realize that
volume, not weight, determined the Indians' choice. In
1730 the committee informed the traders that "in your
Indent for Kettles ... send Us the quantity You would
have each Kettle contain and not the Weight as formerly."[152] Defective goods had to be recorded as untradeable and returned to London.[153] And occasionally the
committee had to educate clerks on the idiosyncrasies of
English weights and measures; for instance, a hundred-
weight of shot was not 100 pounds as a clerk at York had
entered it in the fort account books, but 112 pounds.[154]

Maintaining adequate levels of quality also absorbed
a great deal of the attention of the committee in London.
Historians of the fur trade have long debated who had
superior goods, the French or the English, and what
advantage quality might have given either side.[155] The
question has legitimacy, yet a detailed analysis of the
procurement of trade goods by the Hudson's Bay Company
shows that quality was a factor over which individual
actors, Europeans and Indians, could exert considerable
influence.[156] The company expended much time and money
trying to assure quality, taking special pains to certify
the workmanship of guns. Before placing an order the
committee often had gunsmiths submit samples of their

[151]L.O. to McCliesh, 30 May 1721, HBCA, PAM, A.6/4,
fo. 52d.

[152]L.O. to McCliesh, 30 May 1719, HBCA, PAM, A.6/5,
fo. 36d.

[153]L.O. to Staunton, 28 May 1724, HBCA, PAM, A.6/4,
fo. 86d.

[154]L.O. to McCliesh, 28 May 1723, HBCA, PAM, A.6/4,
fo. 72.

[155]See W. J. Eccles, "A Belated Review of Harold
Adams Innis, The Fur Trade in Canada," Canadian Historical Review 60, no. 4 (1979): 429-34 for an overview of a
half-century of controversy on this issue.

[156]For a discussion of the Indian reaction to quality
see Arthur J. Ray, "Indians as Consumers in the Eighteenth Century," in Ray and Carol M. Judd, Old Trails and
New Directions: Papers of the Third North American Fur
Trade Conference (Toronto: University of Toronto Press,
1980) pp. 255-71.

work,[157] and gunsmiths had to stamp their wares with a trademark so that defective guns could be returned to their makers.[158] Sample guns were kept in the London warehouse to be lent as pattern guns.[159] And before firearms were shipped to the bay, gun surveyors inspected the cargo.[160] Less elaborate though similar procedures were followed to verify the quality of other goods, especially ironwares, which, like guns, had to be stamped with their maker's trademark.[161]

The records of the Hudson's Bay Company indicate that it overcame many of the initial and worst problems with quality. The early minutes and journals frequently mention the return of defective merchandise. Forty-three defective guns and other unsaleable goods were returned in 1679.[162] The 1681 cargo from the bay contained another 122 guns.[163] The following year the traders from Albany returned an even larger batch of merchandise valued at £340.4.0 and containing among other goods almost 15,000 knives.[164] The minutes of the committee do not describe the nature of the defects, whether truly defective or in need of maintenance, but in 1683 much of the returned cargo from Albany Fort was reshipped to York Fort. The company eventually hired gunsmiths to go to the bay to service its own guns and those of the Indians, a move which surely helped to stem the flow of guns from Hudson Bay to London.

There was no one cause of poor quality, but much of the problem could be traced to individual craftsmanship. In 1695 James Knight complained of poor quality guns and determined from the trademarks that those from smiths

---

[157]Minutes, 21 January 1679/80 and 14 November 1681 in Minutes, 1679-1684, vol. 8, pp. 25, 147.

[158]Minutes, 2 February 1679/80, ibid, p. 31.

[159]Minutes, 16 November 1683, ibid, p. 155.

[160]Minutes, 18 May 1681, ibid., p. 123.

[161]Minutes, 2 February 1679/80; 7 December 1683, in ibid., pp. 32, 172.

[162]Minutes, 14 January 1679/80; 2 February 1679/80, in ibid., pp. 22, 31.

[163]Minutes, 20 January 1681/2, in ibid., p. 173.

[164]Minutes, 29 November 1682, in ibid., p. 53.

Lawes and Austine were the offending ones.[165] In other instances poor quality reflected attempts to reduce costs. Knight reported that the guns he received in 1716 were not of the same quality as those he had taken with him in 1714. The committee acknowledged his observation with the assurance that it had begun paying smiths three shillings per gun more to guarantee the necessary quality.[166] A look at the prices the company paid for guns shows that in 1713 and 1714 it paid twenty-one shillings, in 1715 and 1716 twenty shillings, and in 1717 twenty-three shillings, variations undoubtedly resulting from price and quality agreements the company had with its gunsmiths.[167] Quality depended partially on what the company was willing to pay.

Some problems with quality recurred. In the 1700 order for hatchets, committeeman William Potter wrote blacksmith Samuel Banner that the eyes were to be larger than formerly.[168] The 1705 and 1713 orders with Banner contained the same message.[169] But in 1718 and 1724 hatchets with slender eyes were delivered and sent to the bay, much to the dissatisfaction of Indian and trader alike.[170] In 1717 cannon powder was shipped instead of gunpowder.[171] These types of problems can never be eliminated wholly from a commercial enterprise, but the company seems to have learned to minimize them by early in the eighteenth century.

Some of the continual complaining about the quality of metal goods must be attributed to the lack of technology to produce metals which would perform well in

---

[165]L.O. to Knight, 30 May 1696, Letters Outward, vol. 20, p. 270.

[166]L.O. to Knight, 31 May 1717, HBCA, PAM, A.6/4, fo. 11d.

[167]Invoice Book, HBCA, PAM, A.24/2, fos. 32d-33, 37d-38, 60-60d, 67-67d, 81.

[168]Letter, 1 March 1700, HBCA, PAM, A.6/3, fo. 45d.

[169]Letters, 24 February 1705 and 14 February 1713, HBCA, PAM, A.6/3, fos. 66d, 119d.

[170]L.O. to McCliesh, 30 May 1720, HBCA, PAM, A.6/4, fo. 41d.

[171]L.O. to McCliesh, 3 May 1719, HBCA, PAM, A.6/4, fo. 33d.

extreme cold. Jens Munk, the Danish explorer who camped at Churchill during the winter of 1619-20, noted in his journal the hardships that the extreme cold caused him and his men.

> When I had the body of Hans Brook buried ... I ordered that two falconets should be fired in his honour ... But the very sharp frost had made the iron so brittle that the trunnions broke off both weapons when they were discharged with the result that the man who fired them nearly lost his legs.

> On the night of the twenty-eighth [January] the cold was so severe that it burst a tin kettle which the boy had left in the cabin with a little water in it. As tin cannot stand the terrible frosts of such icy seas I don't know what kind of vessels should be used to preserve precious waters in that region.[172]

Even taking into account variations in the quality of iron, many of the problems with metals reflected the state of metal technology rather than poor workmanship or the level of industrialization in any one European country. Complaints about poor quality metal goods need to be judged carefully to determine the origin of the problem, whether it was craftsmanship over which the company had some control or technological and environmental conditions over which it had little or no control.

In addition to urging better quality upon its suppliers, the company also hired blacksmiths who made some small metal goods at the bay. Governor Nixon had suggested this alternative as early as 1682, but the company did not act on it until some years later.[173] The 1690-91 York Fort account book shows that fifty scrapers and twenty-four fish lances were made at the fort.[174] But the accepted practice of making some metal goods at the bay seems to have been arrived at with some give and take between the committee and the traders. In 1702 the committee wrote Governor Fullartine that they had sent no ice chisels, hatchets, or scrapers since he had "forbid" them from doing so. Instead they sent iron, steel,

---

[172]Jens Munk, The Journals of Jens Munk, ed. and intro. W. A. Kenyon (Toronto: Royal Ontario Museum, 1980), p. 28.

[173]Ray, "Indians as Consumers," pp. 258-59.

[174]HBCA, PAM, B.239/d/3, fos. 15d-37.

coals, and another smith.[175]   Table 5 shows that by the early part of the eighteenth century fort production added a significant quantity of goods to the inventory.[176]

Table 5: Trade Goods Produced at Albany Fort, 1715-1725

	1716	1717	1718	1719	1720	1721	1722	1723	1724
Hatchets	450	200	60	400	150	15	100	50	200
Ice Chisels	150	150	250	200	124	200	250	150	150
Mocotogans	40								48
Bayonets	50	150	50	150	36	100	90	100	
Scrapers	60	24	100	30	50	100	150		100
Gunworms	573					100	50		
Guns*				24	25		18		12

*probably gun repairs

Thomas McCliesh wrote the London committee that it was to send no more ice chisels or scrapers, and that the products produced by the fort smiths were preferred by the Indians.   Thus some innovation took place at the bay. The Indian preference for some post-made goods is just one indication.   In 1713 the committee wrote that it wanted to see a sample of a mocotogan, a regular trade item of bayside manufacture.[177]   Who designed this type of curved knife, and when, is unknown, but it was produced at both Albany and York Forts.[178]

The Hudson's Bay Company fully realized that its Indian customers would turn to its French competitors if

[175]L.O. to Fullartine, 1702, HBCA, PAM, A.6/3, fo. 53.

[176]Albany Fort Account Books, HBCA, PAM, B.3/d/24, fo. 14d; B.3/d/25, fo. 4d; B.3/d/26, fo.11d; B.3/d/27, fo. 5d; B.3/d/28, fo. 4d; B.3/d/29, fo. 3d; B.3/d/30, fo. 3d; B.3/d/31, fo. 3d; and B.3/d/32, fo. 3d.

[177]L.O. to Beale, 10 June 1713, HBCA, PAM, A.6/3, fo. 120d.

[178]Arthur J. Ray in "Indians and Consumers" argues that Indians before 1763 were not passive and powerless, as demonstrated by their pressure on the Europeans to produce goods appropriate to their needs.   Indians may have played a technologically innovative role by demanding improved metal goods and firearms (pp. 267-68).   The idea warrants further attention, especially in the area of goods manufactured at the bayside posts.

dissatisfied with the quality of its trade goods. As well, the company could ill afford to have substandard merchandise wasting in its warehouses. Some French goods were superior to English goods. The company could not purchase English flints of a quality equivalent to French flints, and so purchased French flints when it could.[179] French gunpowder was considered superior to English.[180] While it is clear that the Hudson's Bay Company had to import some of its trade goods, most notably French flints and Brazil tobacco from Portugal, the other evidence on the preference of Indians for goods of one nationality over another is very problematic.

High quality by itself did not guarantee the success of any one company or trade good in the fur trade, and the factors that influenced quality were numerous and complex. It was a business problem that demanded continual attention. By the early eighteenth century the Hudson's Bay Company had learned to optimize quality and heed the signs of changed quality. These two management practices contributed more to the company's commercial success than did the umbrella of English industrialism.

Prices for trade goods, unlike the price of beaver, were relatively stable during the first half-century of the company's existence. With modest purchases the company could do little to reduce the price of trade merchandise, except to purchase directly from manufacturers, which it had done from early on, or to lower the quality at the risk of offending the Indians. Table 6 lists the prices for fourteen different items from 1680 to 1728. Prices for metal goods changed little. The price of powder rose sharply at the turn of the century and then declined again. Prices for the two imported items, Brazil tobacco and flints, fluctuated more than those of domestic goods. The decline in the prices of all three cloth items, blankets, broadcloth, and duffel, after the 1720s was offset by a rise in the company's cost of dying and packing cloth, though part of the deline may have been caused by rationalization and growth in this sector of the English economy.

The spotty price data for the early years contrast sharply with the data for the years after 1713. This is

---

[179]L.O. to Beale, 10 June 1713, HBCA, PAM, A.6?3, fo. 120d.

[180]L.O. to Fullartine, 3 June 1705, HBCA, PAM, A.6/3, fo. 70.

56

Table 6: Trade Good Prices in Sterling

Year	Guns /pc.	Kettle /lb.	Hatchet med/pc.	Lg.Roach Knife/dz	Powder /cwt.	Shot /cwt.	Vermillion /oz.
1680		1:3.5			2:14:0		
1681		1:3					
1682	22:6	1:4	-:10	2:2	2:10:0	12:10-14:10	
1683							
1684			-:12				
1685	24:0	1:4	-:12	2:8	2:6:0	12:6-14:6	
1686							
1687	24:0		-:12	2:8	2:9:0	12:0-14:0	
1688							
1689	24:0	1:4					
1690	24:0	1:3.5			3:5:0		
1691	25:0		-:12				
1692							
1693							
1694		1:4				10:6-12:6	
1695	25:0					10:6-12:6	
1696							
1697							
1698	26:0	1:5			2:7:0		
1699		1:5			2:8:0		
1700		1:5					9:0
1701	24:0				3:15:0		
1702	24:0	1:4.5			4:10:0		
1703	24:0						
1704							
1705	24:0	1:3.5	-:10		4:1:0		6:6
1706	24:0				4:0:0		6:6
1707							
1708		1:4.5			3:10:0		7:.75
1709							
1710	24:0	1:4.5			3:15:0		8:0
1711	24:0	1:3			3:5:0		7:6
1712	23:0	1:4			3:5:0		
1713	21:0	1:4	-:11	2:6		10:0	7:6
1714	21:0	1:4	-:10	2:4	3:5:0	11:5	7:6
1715	20:0	1:5	-:10.5	2:6	3:0:0	12:0	6:4
1716	20:0	1:6	-:10.5	2:4	3:5:0	9:6-10:6	7:0
1717	23:0	1:6	-:10	2:1	3:10:0	10:6-13:6	7:0
1718	23:0	1:5	-:9.5	2:4	3:10:0	12:3.5	7:8
1719	23:0	1:5.5	-:10.5	2:4	3:10:0	12:11	8:0
1720	22:0	1:6	-:10	2:4	3:5:0	12:5.5	8:0
1721	22:0	1:6	-:10	2:4	3:5:0	12:8.5	8:0
1722	22:0	1:6	-:11	2:4	3:5:0	12:0-15:0	8:0
1723	22:0	1:5.5	-:11	2:4	3:5:0	12:6-14:6	7:6
1724	22:0	1:5	-:11.5	2:4	3:5:0	15:6-17:6	7:0
1725	22:0	1:5	-:11.5	2:4	3:5:0	15:0-17:0	7:0
1726	22:0	1:5	-:11.5	2:4	3:15:0	15:9-19:6	7:0
1727	22:0	1:5	-:11.5	2:4	4:15:0	15:11.5	7:0
1728	22:0	1:5	-:11.5	2:4	2:18:0	17:.5	7:0

Table 6: cont'd

Year	Flints /1000	Braz'Tob /lb.	Twine /sk.	Comb /pc.	Blankets /pc.	Broadcloth /yd.	Duffel /yd.
1680	5:0					3:10	
1681				-:6.5		3:11	
1682			1:2	-:6	10:9,8:9	3:3.5	
1683							
1684							
1685	3:3.5			-:6		2:11	
1686				-:6.5		3:2-3:9	
1687	2:0:0			-:6.5			
1688							
1689							
1690				-:6			
1691							
1692							
1693							
1694					7:6	3:4	
1695	14:0			-:7			
1696					8:6		
1697					8:6		
1698							
1699							
1700		1:3					
1701		1:3	1:2		6:6		
1702			1:2		6:9	3:2.5	2:6
1703						2:7.5	
1704							
1705		-:11	1:2	-:6.5	6:4	3:4	2:6
1706						3:1	2:6
1707							
1708		2:1				3:1.5	
1709							
1710				-:7			
1711		1:3		-:7.5		3:0	
1712		-:9					2:4.5
1713	10:0	-:9	1:2	-:7	6:1.5	3:9	2:6
1714	7:6	-:11.5	1:2	-:6.5	6:4	3:8.5	2:8
1715	11:0	1:3	1:3	-:6.5	6:4	3:0	2:8
1716		-:10.25	1:2	-:6.5	6:4	3:5.5	2:8
1717		-:10.25	1:2	-:6.25	6:4	3:4	2:8
1718	10:0		1:2	-:6.25	6:6	3:4	2:9
1719	10:0	1:3.5			6:6	3:0	2:9
1720	10:0	1:4	1:2	-:6.5	6:6	3:2.5	2:9
1721	10:0	1:3	1:2	-:6.25	6:6	3:2	2:9
1722	10:0	1:3	1:2	-:6.25	6:4	3:3	2:8
1723		1:3		-:6.25	6:0	2:10	2:6
1724	10:0		1:2	-:6.25	6:0	2:9	
1725	10:0	1:3	1:2	-:6.25	5:8	2:7.5	2:4
1726	10:0	1:0	1:2	-:6.25	5:6	2:4.5	
1727		1:0		-:5	5:2	2:3	1:9
1728		1:2	1:2	-:6.25	4:2	2:5	1:10

due partly to the difficulty of locating prices for some years, and partly to changes in record-keeping.[181] But mostly it reflects irregularities in purchasing. In one year the committee would overstock an item and then not purchase it for two or three years. After 1713 the company learned to turn over this portion of its working capital more regularly. This development complemented the stabilization of the beaver inventory in London. Improved control of both the trade goods and fur inventories provides much of the explanation of why the company started distributing annual dividends in 1718.

One should not discount the importance of the episodes described above. Viewed individually, one was a problem of poor quality, another a problem of ordering, another a problem of bookkeeping. Viewed collectively, each represented a problem related to the acquisition and disposition of the trade inventory. The distance between the source of supply and the source of demand created a disequilibrium which the company learned to correct through bookkeeping, indents, and annual correspondence. The fall in the price of beaver in the 1690s compelled the company to refine further these administrative practices, so as to weather the transition from trading the scarce luxury of fur to trading a more abundant luxury. The large number of Hudson's Bay Company records that discuss problems with the quality and quantity of trade goods illustrate a well run management system and a tightly controlled inventory.

The economical management of the trade goods inventory necessitated an administrative system comprised of bookkeeping and correspondence both in London and North America. The most pedestrian details of quality, quantity, and selection had to be recorded, for this system was the only form of communication possible. The committee in London did not originally recognize the need for such a system. By 1680, however, its basic outlines had begun to emerge. The drop in the price of beaver compelled its refinement; hostilities in Europe and in Hudson Bay postponed its full emergence until 1713 and the Treaty of Utrecht. By 1718 the Hudson's Bay Company shareholders were profiting from the careful attention the committee had given to the economical management of its operation.

---

[181]The price data for the years 1680-1713 were gleaned from the Grand Journals, HBCA, PAM, series A.15; the Grand Ledgers, series A.14; the Minute Books, series A.1; and the Invoice Books, series A.24. From 1714-1726 all prices can be found in the Invoice Books for those years.

Chapter 4

PROBLEMS OF COMMERCE, THE STANDARD OF TRADE AND

ECONOMIC BEHAVIOR IN THE EARLY MODERN PERIOD

The Hudson's Bay Company has bequeathed to posterity one of the more enigmatic price schedules known in world trade. The "Standard of Trade" used by the company in North America expressed the price of European trade goods as a quantity of "made beaver," understood by traders and Indians to be a prime whole beaver pelt.[182] For instance, in 1715 at Albany a gun cost ten pelts, a yard of broadcloth two pelts, and a pound of Brazil tobacco one pelt.[183] Coming into existence within ten years of the company's founding in 1670 and remaining in use for over two centuries, the standard essentially made the beaver pelt the North American currency of the Hudson's Bay Company. The "made beaver" assumed the three functions normally ascribed to money: a medium of exchange, a unit of account, and a store of value.[184] Thus, the standard is one of the best surviving examples of institutionalized barter, theoretically eliminating exchange variability. It is also a striking example of the prolonged use of a non-metallic currency.

---

[182]Arthur J. Ray, Indians in the Fur Trade: Their Role as Hunters, Trappers and Middlemen in the Lands Southwest of Hudson Bay 1660-1870 (University of Toronto Press, 1974) pp. 61-62.

[183]Most account books included a standard at the beginning. For an example see HBCA, PAM, B.3/d/25, fos. 15-15d. Similarly all other furs were valued in terms of "made beaver." For example, four marten to one beaver was a normal HBC equivalent for the two types of furs.

[184]Karl Polanyi, "The Economy as Instituted Process," in George Dalton ed., Primitive, Archaic and Modern Economies: Essays of Karl Polanyi (Garden City, N. J.: Anchor Books, 1968), pp. 166-69. This definition is the one used by Arthur J. Ray and Donald Freeman in 'Give Us Good Measure': An Economic Analysis of Relations Between the Indians and the Hudson's Bay Company Before 1763 (Toronto: University of Toronto Press, 1978), pp. 54-55.

Economic historians of the fur trade have found it particularly puzzling that prices on the standard remained virtually static for nearly two centuries and were revised only occasionally by the committee in London which managed the company. The persistence of static prices in a period of economic growth and in one well-known for its discourses on the relationship between prices and the rhythms of the economy, has left scholars groping for an explanation for this seeming economic paradox. The major hindrance impeding the inquiry is a penchant for explaining this paradox in terms of economic theory rather than in those of historical circumstances. The intent of the following analysis is to place the Standard of Trade in historical perspective.[185]

The static prices on the standard have become a central feature of discussions on the economic motivation and behavior of the North American Indian in the fur trade. E. E. Rich and Abraham Rotstein have suggested that the static prices fundamentally transgress the received wisdom of what constitutes rational economic behavior for Europeans. The logic of their argument is that any economically rational European merchant would want prices to be responsive to supply and demand. If the prices the Hudson's Bay Company paid for furs did not change it was because the company faced an obstacle so insurmountable that it was obliged to adopt behavior that would otherwise be deemed economically irrational. That insurmountable obstacle was Indian economic behavior.[186] Indians, these authors suggest, did not have an economic system guided by market forces; supply and demand did not influence Indian economic decision-making. The exchange of goods within and among Indian communities had social

---

[185]See C. H. Wilson, "The Historical Study of Economic Growth and Decline in Early Modern History," in The Economic Organization of Early Modern Europe, vol. 5, Cambridge Economic History of Europe, eds. E. E. Rich and C. H. Wilson (Cambridge: Cambridge University Press, 1977), for a discussion of the growing transition in economic history towards the development of endogenous theory rather than the borrowing of exogenous theory.

[186]E. E. Rich, "Trade Habits and Economic Motivation Among the Indians of North America," Canadian Journal of Economics and Political Science 26 (1960): 35-53; Abraham Rotstein, "Fur Trade and Empire: An Institutional Analysis" (Ph. D. diss., University of Toronto, 1967), pp. 2, 11, 16, 46, 61; and Rotstein, "Innis: The Alchemy of Wheat and Fur," Journal of Canadian Studies 12 (Winter 1977): 6-31.

and political functions which superseded considerations
of market forces, and the fur trade became a way for
Indians to forge political and military alliances with
Europeans and other Indian groups. The acquisition of
guns from European traders figured largely in that sce-
nario. Only secondarily was trade a way for Indians to
acquire the other European manufactures they desired:
blankets, kettles, knives, hatchets, and other assorted
goods. In this trade, price did not play a determining
role.[187]

This theory of Indian economic behavior has been
challenged by Arthur J. Ray and Donald Freeman. Using a
quantitative analysis of variations in the volume of furs
traded as a ratio of the volume of trade goods, they show
that when competition between French and English traders
increased the Hudson's Bay Company received fewer furs
for the amount of goods traded. This was possible within
the constraints of the rigid standard because the company's traders would inflate the barter prices above
those of the standard, building back into the trade some
flexibility for higgling and haggling. The implication
is that Indians did respond to competition in a manner
associated with the marketplace by demanding more goods
for the amount of furs traded. Barter ratios in the fur
trade were not as static as the standard might lead one
to believe; rather, the standard became the maximum made
beaver price the company would pay for furs.[188]

While Ray and Freeman's analysis effectively cautions
against a facile attribution of the static nature of the
standard to Indian economic behavior, it does not answer
the question of why it remained unchanged for so long.
Simple counterfactual questions may help to identify some
problems of analysis and point towards new avenues of
investigation. Suppose for a moment that prices on the
standard had fluctuated. How then would they have fluctuated? Up? Down? In response to changes in the price
of furs in London? In response to changes in the price
of trade goods in London? In response to both? Where
would all of these decisions have been made? In London?
At the bay posts? And by whom? The Committee in London?
The traders at the bay? And how would all of this infor-

---

[187]This analysis of Indian economic behavior as elaborated by Rotstein is based on Karl Polanyi's theory of
administered trade. See Rotstein, "Fur Trade and Empire," p. 2.

[188]Ray and Freeman, 'Give Us Good Measure', pp. 218-
222 and passim.

mation on prices have been coordinated and disseminated? By slow boat? How else? These were the seventeenth and eighteenth centuries after all.

What this line of questioning illustrates is the magnitude of the logistical problems inherent in long-distance trade during this period. Clear-sighted decision-making was exceedingly difficult, if not at times impossible. The task of responding rationally to supply and demand fluctuations without full and accurate information plagued merchants in all sectors of the pre-industrial economy, but none so acutely as those dealing in long-distance trade.[189] Living in an age in which a flood of information threatens to consume us we often overlook the ways in which a lack of information forced a different ordering of affairs in bygone times. It is one of the missing pieces to understanding the Standard of Trade not just as an economic phenomenon but also as a historical phenomenon.

The Standard of Trade, a price schedule using the beaver pelt as the unit of value, evokes more primitive times, an anachronism lingering on in the industrializing nineteenth-century world because the fur trade supposedly remained on the fringe of that economic order. Rich and others have construed this method of transacting business as an outcome of the meeting of the Indian and European during England's commercial expansion in the seventeenth century. Trading practices coalesced from a union of two dissimilar cultures, and the standard represented a European accommodation to the Indian.[190] This construc-

---

[189]Barry Supple, "The Nature of Enterprise," in The Economic Organization of Early Modern Europe, pp. 394, 396-7, 407-8, 439. The impact of market uncertainty on entrepreneurial undertakings is a major theme in much of the recent economic history, especially that dealing with long-distance trade. See Bernard Bailyn, "Communications and Trade: The Atlantic in the Seventeenth Century," Journal of Economic History, 13 (1953): 380; J. M. Sosin, English America and the Restoration Monarchy of Charles II (University of Nebraska Press, 1980) pp. 5-23; Niels Steensgaard, Carracks, Caravans and Companies (Odense, Denmark: Studentlitterature Andelsbogtrykkeriet, 1973) pp. 7, 10, 114; and Ian K. Steele, The English Atlantic, 1675-1740: An Exploration of Communication and Community (Oxford University Press, 1986), passim.

[190]Rotstein, "Innis: The Alchemy of Wheat and Fur," p. 12; Rich, "Trade Habits and Economic Motivation," p. 42; and Ray and Freeman, 'Give Us Good Measure', pp. 54-55.

tion is, however, ahistorical, the shadow of the present darkening the past, for the standard has its roots as much in the economic world of seventeenth-century Europe as in the economic world of seventeenth-century North American Indians. This is not to suggest that the European and native North American economic cultures are readily comparable, had the same needs, or moved to the same rhythms. It is to say that for the seventeenth-century European the Standard of Trade was not atavistic, but rather was a creative response to structural problems intrinsic to the economy of the time.

To demonstrate that the standard has a historical dimension as well as an economic dimension derived from a European context, it is necessary to look beyond the North American fur trade to the larger European commercial world. From this vantage point it is possible to appreciate better two major characteristics of the standard: one, the way in which it formalized barter trade and two, its setting of prices. Both practices had precedents in European commerce predating the Hudson's Bay Company.

Barter trade and furs share a long, intertwined history. Permanence of value, durability, and ease of transport made sable a medium of exchange in cash-poor but fur-rich Russia. In early Kievan Russia and Novgorod, furs circulated as a currency and when used as such were referred to by the specialized word kuny, an old Russian word for marten. By the fifteenth century furs were no longer valued in terms of themselves but in terms of a metallic currency; nonetheless, Russians used them as a substitute for cash for another two centuries. In the first half of the seventeenth century the tsar established the Sable Treasury as a branch of the Siberian Department. When supplies of precious metals ran low the state would discharge its debts with sable. Foreign merchants to Russia frequently received payment in furs, and the state remunerated foreigners for their services with furs.[191]

In western Europe furs did not play a key function in the economy as they did in Russia, in part because by the Middle Ages wild furbearing animals had been greatly reduced in numbers and their habitats encroached upon by

---

[191]Raymond H. Fisher, The Russian Fur Trade, 1550-1700 (Berkeley: University of California Press, 1943) pp. 8-9, 123, 129-30.

settlement.[192]   Soon after arriving in North America, however, European settlers discovered furs to be one commodity which could be readily acquired and easily marketed, thereby generating the necessary earnings to purchase the European goods they needed.   Obtained from the Indians by bartering European goods and hence requiring a minimal amount of labor, furs were an ideal commodity to undergird the economies of the labor-intensive agricultural settlements of the Atlantic seaboard.   There is a paucity of information on the pedestrian details of how this trade was organized, but some traders evidently evolved methods of regularizing barter trade which bore marked similarity to the practices of the Hudson's Bay Company.   Evert Wendell, a New York trader, sketched beavers in his account book to record credit transactions with Indian customers.[193]   The Pynchons in Massachusetts subcontracted their monopoly trading rights to others with the proviso that traders would buy trading goods from the Pynchon store paid for in beaver.[194]

Barter persisted as a common and accepted method of trade well into the eighteenth century both in Europe and the Americas.   In international trade, merchants had long used barter to grease the wheels of commerce in the absence of hard cash and because of an understandable lack of faith in paper money and bills of exchange. Glasgow merchants transacted much of their trade with West Africa and the West Indies on a barter basis well into the eighteenth century.[195]   The Baltic ports often offered no alternative to barter.   Unable to obtain cash payments for furs shipped to Russia between 1694 and 1710, the Hudson's Bay Company accepted payment in Russian commodities: hog bristles, dressed hides, potash, tallow, yarn, but mostly hemp which it then flogged to

---

[192]Elspeth M. Veale, The English Fur Trade in the Later Middle Ages (Oxford: Oxford University Press, 1966) p. 59.

[193]Thomas Elliot Norton, The Fur Trade in Colonial New York, 1686-1776 (Madison: University of Wisconsin Press, 1974) pp. 29-30.

[194]Francis X. Moloney, The Fur Trade in New England, 1620-1676 (Cambridge: Harvard University Press, 1931) pp. 56-57.

[195]C. H. Wilson, "Trade, Society and the State," in The Economic Organization of Early Modern Europe, p. 513; and Herman van der Wee, "Monetary, Credit and Banking Systems," ibid., pp. 306-7.

the Lords of the Admiralty.[196] Throughout Europe much of the trade in small local centers was barter; people living in the countryside seldom saw coins, and even more seldom used them.[197]

In bullion-starved colonial North America metal-based currencies served as a unit of value and a unit of account, but only erratically as a medium of exchange. Colonials transacted most of their business as barter which took two forms: truck barter with a simultaneous exchange of goods, and bookkeeping barter which allowed for a time-lag by extending credit. Surviving account books from the period suggest that small colonial merchants utilized bookkeeping primarily to lubricate the mechanism of barter trade, facilitating complex and extended exchange in the absence of circulating currency. Instructions for methods of recording barter transactions warranted a separate chapter in the sixth edition of John Mair's Bookkeeping Modernized printed in 1793.[198] Throughout the colonies merchants extended credit in the form of European imports and received payment in colonial commodities.[199] In some instances, wages were calculated in commodities. Christopher Jeaffreson, a planter and merchant in the West Indies, paid wages in sugar. In 1681 he considered competent tailors, coopers, joiners, carpenters, masons, and smiths worth a thousand pounds of sugar a year; indentured servants received four hundred pounds of sugar at the end of a minimum four-year term of

---

[196]E. E. Rich, The Hudson's Bay Company, 1670-1870, vol. 1: 1670-1763 (London: Hudson's Bay Record Society, 1958), pp. 398, 461.

[197]F. P. Braudel and F. Spooner, "Prices in Europe from 1540 to 1750," in The Economy of Expanding Europe in the 16th and 17th Centuries, vol. 4, Cambridge Economic History of Europe, eds. E. E. Rich and C. H. Wilson (Cambridge: Cambridge University Press, 1967), p. 377.

[198]W. T. Baxter, "Accounting in Colonial America," in A. C. Littleton and B. S. Yamey, eds., Studies in the History of Accounting (Homewood, Illinois: Richard D. Irwin, Inc., 1956), pp. 272-75, 278.

[199]Letter from Christopher Jeaffreson, St. Christopher's Island to Mr. Poyntz, London, June 5, 1676, in Seventeenth-Century Economic Documents, eds. Joan Thirsk and J. P. Cooper (Oxford: Clarendon Press, 1972), p. 544.

service.[200] Throughout the British American colonies taxes were frequently collected in the major commodity of the region and public debts were discharged with those same commodities. In the 1731 accounts for St. Mark's Parish, Virginia, both debits and credits are entered in pounds of tobacco without metallic currency equivalents.[201]

Thus, the practice of barter trade by the Hudson's Bay Company was an accommodation to the prevailing economic conditions of the time as much as it was an accommodation to the economic attitudes and practices of the Indians. In fact, it simplified the company's operations by letting it skirt entirely the thorny and controversial issue of bullion transfers. Moreover, in view of the prevalence and acceptance of barter, it is not particularly surprising that the Hudson's Bay Company established prices to control it.

Understanding the role of fixed prices in pre-industrial strategies and planning, whether in a barter economy or a fully monetized economy, is important enough to rehearse briefly some highlights of its historical development. In the Letters Outward, the annual HBC correspondence from London to the traders at the bay, the committee frequently admonished the traders to adhere to the standard. Some have noted that this emphasized the employee status of the HBC traders, in contrast to the flexibility and independence enjoyed by French traders. E. E. Rich suggested that because of this, "the French ... could make a generous bargain in order to attract trade and then drive hard terms to take advantage of the opportunities." This analysis needs to be tempered and qualified; the flexibility of the French was not necessarily an advantage or even universally present, nor was the constraint on trade imposed by the HBC standard necessarily a handicap.[202]

Again we return to the problem of the relationship between information and rational economic decision-making. Profitable results from higgling and haggling

_____

[200]Letter from Christopher Jeaffreson, St. Christopher's Island to Mr. Poyntz, London, May 5, 1681, ibid., p. 549.

[201]St. Mark's Parish Vestry Book, 1730-1785, Rosalie E. Davis, ed. (Manchester, Mo.: private printing, 1983) p. 51.

[202]Rich, H.B.C., 1670-1870, vol. 1, pp. 75-76.

require relatively good market information. In an ideal marketplace sellers know, at least, the minimum price their goods must command in order to cover expenses. The Hudson's Bay Company traders, hired to conduct the fur trade in the absence of the shareholders, lacked the information necessary to calculate a base price. Without this information, the prospect of trading at unprofitable prices increased dramatically. The Montreal traders' suppleness and independence which allowed them to take advantage of opportunities may have been the undoing of many. With little or no information about the European market, offers which appeared to them as opportunities may instead have been costly illusions.

The greater the distance between markets, the less reliable the information which coordinated those markets. The ability of merchants to organize their affairs so as to mitigate the problems caused by inadequate information often spelled the difference between success and failure. A number of measures recommended themselves. Bookkeeping, correspondence, and profit incentives were administrative procedures frequently employed.[203] As well, the employment of reliable and trustworthy factors to prosecute the trade in the absence of the owners was crucial. Employment of kin was one means by which a merchant could secure a personal commitment from his agents. The American colonial trade, dominated by individually-owned firms or small partnerships, evolved a transatlantic commercial network held together by the bonds of kinship and long acquaintance.[204] A similar pattern typified the eighteenth-century Montreal fur trade.[205]

In some circumstances merchants adopted price-fixing, another mechanism of control, which created market information in its absence. One of the aims of the early regulatory companies, organizations of merchants trading overseas to areas specified by charter, was to control the volume of trade and to set minimum prices for goods in hopes of tempering violent fluctuations in price and supply. In 1599 a group of merchants trading in the Levant agreed on a minimum price for the

---

[203]Supple, "The Nature of Enterprise," p. 417.

[204]Bailyn, "Communications and Trade," p. 380; and J. M. Sosin, English America, pp. 5-23.

[205]Jennifer S. H. Brown, Strangers in Blood: Fur Trade Company Families in Indian Country (Vancouver: University of British Columbia Press, 1980), pp. 35-50.

English kersey sold to Turkish merchants; the agreement became unenforceable when one merchant evaded the letter of the contract by bartering kersey for indigo. A 1626 agreement proved more successful, incorporating restrictions on barter.[206] Joint-stock companies, whose supply markets were protected by royal charter from competition with their own nationals, were most successful in fixing prices. Because competition in the domestic and overseas markets was never wholly absent, companies tended to favor moderate but stable prices to achieve long-term control of the market over high prices and short-term profits.[207] The establishment of fixed prices by the Hudson's Bay Company for its North American sphere of trade conformed to the entrepreneurial practices of other joint-stock companies. It created information, reduced uncertainty, and increased market transparency.[208]

One aspect of Indian economic behavior, tangentially related to the above issues, warrants brief mention before proceeding to a more detailed analysis of the Standard of Trade. Arthur J. Ray, Donald Freeman, and others have noted that fluctuations in the barter price of trade goods did not influence significantly the consumer habits of the Indian and the production of furs. Indians had relatively inelastic consumption patterns and produced furs sufficient to fill their needs. If Europeans had offered a higher price for furs, and hence a lower price for trade goods, the production of furs would have fallen. Competitive conditions influenced the flow of goods whether to the French or to the English but lower prices for trade goods did not increase the production of furs. Rich and Rotstein argued that because fluctuations in price did not affect production the price mechanism did not work, and that the fur trade was therefore not a true market economy.[209] Ray and Freeman con-

---

[206]Niels Steensgaard, "Consuls and Nations in the Levant from 1570 to 1650," Scandinavian Economic History Review 15, no. 1 (1967): 45-46.

[207]Niels Steensgaard, Carracks, Caravans and Companies, pp. 47, 142-43, 152.

[208]Market transparency refers to the degree of information available for decision making purposes. The greater the amount of information the greater the transparency or clarity in the market.

[209]Rich, "Trade Habits and Economic Motivation," pp. 42, 48-48, 52-53; and Rotstein, "Innis: The Alchemy of Wheat and Fur," pp. 12, 16.

cluded that because Indians did respond to competitive prices then market forces were operating.[210] All, however, left the theoretical issue of the relationship between price and production in abeyance.

The difficulty arises from an over-simplification of the correlation between price mechanisms, markets, and production, as if they constituted an indivisible whole. They subsume two phenomena, related yet distinguishable one from the other. The first is the short-term interplay of prices and the market, where competitive behavior is observed. This is the behavior of subarctic Indians which Ray and Freeman demonstrated in 'Give Us Good Measure'. The second is the long-term economic and social relationship between what transpires in the marketplace and the future production decisions of the market participants. This reasoning derives from economic theory, which holds that if competitive prices are functioning then there will be incentive to produce more. When the two are differentiated it becomes possible to reconcile the observed behavior of the Indians as shrewd and hard bargainers, with their inelastic consumption patterns. Historians examining medieval economies have discovered markedly similar economic behavior; both Indians and medieval Europeans were responsive to competitive conditions, yet exhibited relatively constant consumption patterns. The behavior of both raises the question of what precipitates the transition from a non-growth to a growth economy, yet cautions against the hasty answer of price mechanisms. The historical record points towards the need to examine with care the ways in which social, cultural, and political factors impinge upon long-term development of economic structures and economic behavior.

The Standard of Trade, when viewed from a perspective of economic history rather than from the more narrow perspective of fur trade history or economic theory, was not simply an accommodation of economically sophisticated Europeans to "primitive" Indians. It was a mechanism which responded to structural weaknesses in the European economy engendered by the shortage of metallic currencies and by the difficulties of coordinating markets in long-distance trade. It is in this light that a systematic analysis of the standard will be cast.

---

[210]Ray and Freeman, 'Give Us Good Measure', pp. 218-28.

Chapter 5

PRICES, MARK-UPS AND THE STANDARD OF TRADE

The Hudson's Bay Company Standard of Trade was a creative response to the constraints of long-distance trade in the early modern period. The distance separating London and the bay precluded a pricing system based on coordinating supply and demand markets, and the standard established them in their absence. As a price list the Standard of Trade also represented a structure of value, both to the committee in London and the Indians. But to modern students of the fur trade it is virtually meaningless as a structure of value related to anything but itself. Ten beaver pelts for a gun, one for a half pound of Brazil tobacco, and two for a yard of broadcloth express little more than equivalencies of European manufactures for furs. No measure of gain or value by either Indians or Europeans is readily discernable. Yet despite its enigmatic quality for modern scholars it did represent, for the committee in London, the difference between the price the company paid for trade goods and the price it received for furs sold in England. Numerous references in letters to the bayside traders indicate that the London committee was clearly aware of the relationship between the two. In 1702 it wrote to Governor Fullartine at Albany that it was sending only longer guns "by reason that the Standard upon short Guns would not answer the first Cost of them."[211] In 1712, the committee urged Governor Beale to raise the standard on cloth and guns, again arguing that the price of beaver was so low that it would not cover the cost of guns and cloth from the supplier.[212]

---

[211]Letter Outward (hereafter L.O.) to Fullartine, 1702, HBCA, PAM, A.6/3, fo. 52d. "First cost" is a term used in a context which seems to indicate that it meant costs which could be attributed directly to supplying a good. With guns this would include the gun, the gun chests for shipping, and the cost of paying a gun surveyor to inspect the cargo before shipment.

[212]L.O. to Beale, 23 May 1712, HBCA, PAM, A.6/3, fo. 116d.

The company's profit was derived from the difference
between the price it paid for trade goods and the price
it received for furs on the London market, less all expenses.   At various times both critics and scholars of
the Hudson's Bay Company have discussed the company's
profits in terms of the mark-ups on its goods.   E. E.
Rich in his treatment of the mid-eighteenth century parliamentary inquiry of the company concluded that "there
was nothing revealed which approached a profit of two
thousand per cent," as the company's critics had charged,
by noting that the mark-up on guns in 1749 was around 175
percent.[213]   The problem with this approach is that the
gun was just one of dozens of trade goods. One must
question whether it was a good proxy for all trade goods.
Rich chose the gun for his example but the company's
eighteenth-century critic may have been using another
trade good for his example.   What Rich did for guns needs
to be done for all trade goods.

Since the price of trade goods and the price of furs
in England were expressed in pounds sterling, it is possible to convert the prices on the Standard of Trade from
'made beaver' values to sterling values, and thereby calculate mark-ups.   This conversion sheds some light on the
position of the committee in London, as well as making
the standard more amenable to quantitative analysis vis-
a-vis prices of trade goods and furs in England.   The
results of that exercise are the major focus of this
chapter.

The amount of data involved in transcribing the standard is very considerable.   First, the price of fifty-
seven trade goods must be ferreted out of the records.
Partial results of that research have been presented in
Table 6, pages 56 and 57.   Very briefly, Table 6 shows
that the prices of trade goods fluctuated relatively
little over the period from 1670 to 1730, with the exception of imported goods such as Brazil tobacco and flints.
Second, the prices the company received for beaver on the
London market are also necessary, and have been presented
in Table 3, page 36.   With sterling prices for furs and
trade goods available for much of a fifty-year span it is
possible to convert the standard to sterling values for
those years.   The task would be very cumbersome and not
necessarily worth the effort.   For present purposes I
judged both the sterling and made beaver prices for trade
goods to be relatively constant for this period, and

---

[213]E. E. Rich, The History of the Hudson's Bay Company, 1670-1870, vol. 1:1670-1763 (London: Hudson's Bay
Record Society, 1958) p. 594.

sterling prices for beaver variable. What this means is that changes in the sterling value of the standard, and changes in the mark-ups of trade goods sold to the Indians, move in relationship to changes in the price of furs. With a time series for fur prices it is possible to gain a general picture of how the mark-ups on trade goods changed over time, based on a conversion of the standard for one year.

The year for which I have chosen to convert the Standard of Trade from made beaver to sterling values is 1720. It seems an appropriate choice for three reasons. First, it represents a period of stability. In 1713 the French returned York Fort to the English, and in 1714 James Knight reestablished the Hudson's Bay Company's trade there. In 1718 the company began to distribute annual dividends which signalled a period of prosperity. Thus 1720 was a year of stability and prosperity. Second, in this period of stability and after the establishment of York Fort and Fort Churchill, the purchasing of trade goods is fairly regular, and the data on the prices of trade goods fall almost all within 1720. Third, the beaver prices in London were relatively stable, so that the mark-ups calculated on trade goods represent a pattern lasting at least a decade.

The mark-ups for goods at Albany Fort and York Fort range from a low of 45 percent on shoes at Albany to a high of 8300 percent for egg boxes at York, and demonstrate that the mark-up on no one good serves as a suitable proxy for all others. The mark-ups for all goods are given further below in Tables 8a and 8b. But before moving to a discussion of the meaning of the differences it is useful to put each in perspective by weighting the mark-ups as a percentage of total trade in any one year. This I did for Albany for the years 1715-16 through 1725-26 and the results are presented in Table 7.

Table 7: Weighted Average Mark-up, Albany Fort

1715-16	493%	1721-22	443%
1716-17	465%	1722-23	403%
1717-18	445%	1723-24	459%
1718-19	456%	1724-25	408%
1719-20	474%	1725-26	406%
1720-21	464%		

Although the weighted average mark-ups on goods at Albany Fort were substantial, it does show that a sizeable percentage of the trade was in goods with the lower mark-

ups and not on those with the extremely high mark-ups.[214]
The average mark-up on goods at Albany Fort was very
likely high enough to yield the company a profit. Lest
readers lack a comparative frame of reference and be
outraged by these figures, let me note that if they went
into a shop in Montreal or Minneapolis or Moose Jaw and
bought a kettle or a knife or a hatchet manufactured in
England the price would be over 300 percent above the
cost from the factory. And the costs absorbed by that
300 percent mark-up, such as shipping, duty, labor, distribution, and warehousing, would only include one trip
across the Atlantic rather than two which is included in
the mark-ups of the Hudson's Bay Company. But, I stress,
these figures of 400 percent and above are weighted
average mark-ups, not profit. The profit the company
realized is what remained after it paid all of its
expenses including shipping, duties, wages, maintenance
on its trading posts, warehouses in London, and provisions to feed its men. The cost of the trade goods was
only one part of its overall expenses. To judge by the
figures, they were one-fifth to one-quarter of total
receipts.

The mark-ups on individual items are given in Tables
8a and 8b. On these tables the first column is the trade
good. Column two is the price the company paid for the
good in London. The made beaver price of trade goods
taken from the standard is in column three. The fourth
column is the made beaver price expressed in sterling.
The value for one made beaver is 5s.6d., the average
price the company received for beaver from 1716 to 1726
inclusive. An average is used to smooth out some of the
minor fluctuations in beaver prices. The fifth column is
the mark-up on trade goods, calculated as the percentage
increase of the income realized over the initial cost.
For example, in 1720 the company bought guns in London at
22 shillings each, which it sold at York Fort for 14
beaver pelts. The company then sold those furs for
5s.6d. per pelt or £3:17:0 for all 14 pelts, making a
250 percent mark-up over the 22 shillings the company
paid gunsmiths for the guns.

---

[214]Albany Account Books, HBCA, PAM, B/3/d/24, fo.
19d; B/3/d/25, fo. 11d; B/3/d/26 fos. 16-16d; B/3/d/27,
fos. 9d-10; B/3/d/28, fos. 10d-11; B.3/d/29, fos. 9d-
10; B.3/d/30, fos. 9d-10; B.3/d/31, fos. 10-10d;
B.3/d/32, fos. 9d-10; B.3/d/33, fos. 11d-12; B.3/d/34,
fos. 9-9d. The trading year went from July of one year
through June of the next. Thus the figures for 1715-16
represent only a twelve-month trading period.

Table 8a: Standard of Trade Conversion, 1720, York Fort

Trade Goods	Suppliers' Price	Standard	Sterling	% Mark-up	
Thread, lb.	2:0	1/1 MB	5:6	175	[1719]
Guns, pc.	22:0	1/14	3:17:0	250	
Shirt, pc.	2:9	1/2	11:0	300	
Duffel, yd.	2:9	1/2	11:0	300	
Shoes, pr.	3:10	1/3	6:7	330	[1717]
Hawk Bells, pc.	1:2 /12 pc.	12/1	5:6	371	+
Twine, sk.	1:2	1/1	5:6	371	
Sm. Beads, lb.	2:2	1/2	11:0	408	
Broadcloth, yd.	3:2.5	1/3	16:6	414	
Kettles, lb.	1:6	1/1.5	8:3	450	
Blankets, pc.	6:6	1/7	1:18:6	492	
Hatchets, pc.	:10	1/1	5:6	560	+
Sword Blades, pc.	:10	1/1	5:6	560	[1723]
Roll Tobacco, lb.	:9	1/1	5:6	633	
Brandy, gal.	3:0	1/4	1:02:0	633	
Knives, pc.	:2.25	4/1	5:6	633	+
Brazil Tob., lb.	1:4	1/2	11:0	725	
Breast Button, pc.	:8 /72 pc.	72/1	5:6	725	[1718]
Coat Button, pc.	:8 /48 pc.	48/1	5:6	725	
Baize, yd.	:11.25	1/1.5	8:4	780	
Bath Ring, pc.	:1.25	6/1	5:6	780	[1715]
Socks, pr.	1:6	1/2.5	13:10	817	[1718]
Powder, lb.	:7	1/1	5:6	843	
Gloves, pr.	:7	1/1	5:6	843	[1717]
Lg. Beads, lb.	2:2	1/4	1:02:0	915	
Flannel, yd.	:9.5	1/1.5	8:4	942	
Ivory Comb, pc.	:6.25	1/1	5:6	956	+
Spoons, pc.	:6.25 /2 pc.	2/1	5:6	956	[1718]
Seal Ring, pc.	:2	3/1	5:6	1000	
Vermillion, oz.	:6	1/1	5:6	1000	
Scraper	:3	2/1	5:6	1000	[1722]
Shot, lb.	:1.25	4/1	5:6	1220	[1719]
Powder Horn, pc.	:5	1/1	5:6	1220	
Looking Glass, pc.	:5	1/1	5:6	1220	
File, pc.	:5	1/1	5:6	1220	
Fire Steel, pc.	:3.5 /4 pc.	4/1	5:6	1786	
Gun Worm, pc.	:3.3 /4 pc.	4/1	5:6	1900	
Horn Comb, pc.	:1.5	2/1	5:6	2100	
Gartering, yd.	:2.75/1.5 yd	1.5/1	5:6	2300	
Scissors, pr.	:1.3	2/1	5:6	2438	
Tobacco tongs, pr.	:1.3	2/1	5:6	2438	
Awl, pc.	:2.5 /8 pc.	8/1	5:6	2540	
Tobacco box, pc.	:2.5	1/1	5:6	2540	
Thimble, pc.	:2.25 /6 pc.	6/1	5:6	2833	
Flint, pc.	:2 /16 pc.	16/1	5:6	3200	
Needle, pc.	:1.5 /12 pc.	12/1	5:6	4300	+[1719]
Egg Box, pc.	:0.75 /3 pc.	3/1	5:6	8700	
Mocotogan, pc.	@	4/1			
Ice Chisel, pc.	@	1/1			
Net Lines, pc.	@	1/1			

Table 8b: Standard of Trade Conversion, 1720, Albany Fort

Trade Good	Suppliers' Price	Standard	Sterling	% Mark-up	
Shoes, pr.	3:10	1/1 MB	5:6	43	[1717]
3 ft. Gun, pc.	22:0	1/7	1:18:6	75	
Pistol, pc.	12:6	1/4	1:02:0	76	[1718]
Bayonet, pc.	1:6	2/1	5:6	83	
Shirt, pc.	2:9	1/1	5:6	100	
3.5 ft. Gun, pc.	22:0	1/8	2:04:0	100	
4 ft. Gun, pc.	22:0	1/10	2:15:0	150	
Red Feathers	1:0	2/1	5:6	175	[1718]
Hatchet, pc.	:10	2/1	5:6	230	+
Hawk Bell, pc.	1:6 /16 pc.	16/1	5:6	230	+
Sword Blade, pc.	:10	2/1	5:6	230	[1723]
Beads, lb.	2:2	.75/1	5:6	238	
Broadcloth, yd.	3:2.5	1/2	11:0	243	
Socks, pr.	1:6	1/1	5:6	267	[1718]
Kettles, lb.	1:6	1/1	5:6	267	
Knife, pc.	:2.25	8/1	5:6	267	+
Duffel, yd.	2:9	1/2	11:0	300	
Goggles, pr.	:8	2/1	5:6	313	
Brazil Tob., lb.	1:4	1/1	5:6	313	
Twine, sk.	1:2	1/1	5:6	371	
Roll Tobacco, lb.	:9	1.5/1	5:6	389	
Blanket, pc.	6:6	1/6	1:13:2	408	
Spoon, pc.	1:.5 /4 pc.	4/1	5:6	426	
Ivory Comb, pc.	:6.25	2/1	5:6	428	
Coat Button, pc.	1:0 /72 pc.	72/1	5:6	450	
Thread, lb.	2:0	1/2	11:0	450	
Baize, yd.	:11.25	1/1	5:6	487	
Powder, lb.	:7	1.5/1	5:6	529	
Looking Glass, pc.	:5	2/1	5:6	560	
Powder Horn, pc.	:5	2/1	5:6	560	
Keg, 1 gal., pc.	:10	1/1	5:6	560	[1724]
Flannel, yd.	:9.5	1/1	5:6	595	
Keg, 2 gal., pc.	1:2	1/1.5	8:3	608	[1724]
Brandy, gal.	3:0	1/4	1:02:1	633	
Vermillion, oz.	:6	1.5/1	5:6	633	
Leaf Tobacco, lb.	:5.5	1.5/1	5:6	697	[1719]
Breast Button, pc.	:8 /72 pc.	72/1	5:6	725	[1718]
Bath Ring, pc.	:1.25	6/1	5:6	780	[1715]
Gloves, pr.	:7	1/1	5:6	843	[1717]
Laced Hat, pc.	2:3.5	1/4	1:02:0	863	[1718]
Shot, lb.	:1.25	5/1	5:6	956	[1719]
Seal Ring, pc.	:2	3/1	5:6	1000	
Scraper, pc.	:3	2/1	5:6	1000	[1722]
File, pc.	:5	1/1	5:6	1220	
Tobacco Box, pc.	:2.5	2/1	5:6	1220	
Gartering, yd.	:3.75 /2 yd.	2/1	5:6	1660	
Awl, pc.	:3.75 /12 pc.	12/1	5:6	1660	
Fire Steel, pc.	:3.5 /4 pc.	4/1	5:6	1786	
Gun Worm, pc.	:3.3 /4 pc.	4/1	5:6	1900	

Table 8b - con't

Fish Hook, pc.	:3 /20 pc.	20/1	5:6	2100	
Lead, lb.	:3	1/1	5:6	2100	[1718]
Tobacco Tongs, pr.	:1.3	2/1	5:6	2438	
Scissors, pr.	:1.3	2/1	5:6	2438	
Flint, pc.	:2.5 /20 pc.	20/1	5:6	2540	
Thimble, pc.	:2.2 /6 pc.	6/1	5:6	2833	
Needle, pc.	:1.5 /12 pc.	12/1	5:6	4300	+[1719]
Egg Box, pc.	:1 /4 pc.	4/1	5:6	6500	
Net Lines, pc.	@	2/1			
Ice Chisel, pc.	@	2/1			
Mocotogan, pc.	@	2/1			

Key: 0:0:0   pounds: shillings: pence
        +   avg. of more than one price and size
        @   made at the fort
   [year]   price of trade good in that year

No overhead costs are calculated into these figures,
neither of a general nature such as shipping, storage, or
wages, nor of a specific nature such as gun chests or the
preparation of cloth.   Between 1713 and 1728 the cost of
gun chests and the examination of the guns before they
left London added another two to three percent onto the
cost of guns from the supplier.   During the same period
cloth dying and packaging cost the company between 6.6
percent and 48 percent over the initial cost from the
supplier.[215]   Because these costs are difficult to break
down into unit cost and to add to the cost from the
supplier, only the price from the supplier is given.

What the figures in Tables 8a and 8b show most clearly
is a wide discrepancy in the mark-ups.   Within this wide
range some interesting patterns emerge.   Those goods
which were some of the most important trade items and to
which the Indians gave the greatest attention to quality
-- guns, metal goods, and cloth -- also had some of the
lower mark-ups.   It is reasonable to suggest that, in
part, the lower mark-ups on these items were to attract
the trade and to combat French competition.   In 1688 the
committee advised Governor Geyer to keep "to the Standard
that Mr. Radissone agreed to, but withall to give the
Indians all manner of Content and Satisfaction and in

---

[215]These figures have been calculated using the figures of charges on merchandise found in the Invoice
Books, HBCA, PAM, A.24/2-A.24/3.   The cost of gun chests,
the viewing of guns, and the dying and packing of cloth
comprised these charges.

Some goods Under Sell the French that they may be incour-
aged to Come to our Factorys."[216]   Three years later
Thomas Walsh was told to treat the Indians "with all
Kindness Imaginable & to assure them of good wares
cheaper then the French can give them."[217]

These orders to Governors Geyer and Walsh indicate
that in the early years of the company's existence the
committee tried to use prices to attract the Indians to
trade. An analysis of mark-ups of trade goods shows that
the standard built in competitive prices on some goods.
The issue of competitive prices on some trade goods
created tension between the committee in London and John
Nixon, one of its early governors. Nixon assumed command
of the bayside operations in 1679, and shortly thereafter
altered the standard to the displeasure of the committee.
The extent of his transgressions is not known, but the
committee did note that he had lowered the price of guns
and had revalued marten skins as four equal to one beaver, down from the previous eight to one. (It is note-
worthy that the prices on guns and marten, both of which
remained under considerable pressure for the period 1670-
1730, were singled out for mention.) Nixon was recalled
and his successor Henry Sergeant was ordered to reinstate
the standard used by Bayly.[218] It appears that Sergeant
was unable to effect the desired changes because in 1685
the committee sent Pierre Radisson to the bay as "Chief
Director of ... Trade at Port Nellson ... and to promote
the interest of the Company & Settle a Standard of Commerce with the Natives."[219] Radisson's efforts seem to
have quieted the committee for it advised Governor Geyer
to adhere to the standard which Radisson had set.[220]

What Radisson accomplished is unclear as no trading
records survive from that period. Later at York Fort
(Port Nelson), guns cost the Indians ten pelts for a

---

[216]L.O. to Geyer, 2 June 1688, in Letters Outward,
1688-1696, ed. E. E. Rich (London: Hudson's Bay Record
Society, vol. 20) p. 14.

[217]L.O. to Thomas Walsh, 21 May 1691, ibid., p. 128.

[218]L.O. to Sergeant, 16 May 1684, in Letters Outward,
1679-1694, ed. E. E. Rich (London: Hudson's Bay Record
Society, vol. 11, 1948) pp. 120-21.

[219]L.O. to Radisson, 22 May 1685, ibid., p. 147.

[220]L.O. to Geyer, 2 June 1688, in Letters Outward,
vol. 20, p. 14.

"short" gun and twelve for a "long" gun,[221] as the committee desired, but marten remained valued at four to one beaver.[222]   At Albany, where Nixon had committed his transgressions, guns were valued between six and twelve beaver in 1689,[223] below the nine to twelve pelts recommended to Sergeant in 1684.[224]   Thus Radisson did not rectify Nixon's two recorded errors.   During this period the company's shareholders shifted from being predominantly members of the court to being merchants and city men.   The latter may have been willing to accept low prices on goods which came under price pressure -- such as guns and marten -- and to regain the difference on other trade goods, a hypothesis made more credible by the letters of 1688 and 1691 advising the traders to undersell the French on some goods.

The strategy of using goods to attract the trade is clearest with guns.   Guns had much lower mark-ups than their necessary accessories.   At York Fort the mark-up was 250 percent for guns but 843, 1200, 1220, and 1900 percent respectively for powder, shot, powder horns, and gunworms.   At Albany the pattern was similar; 75, 100, and 150 percent mark-ups on guns, and 529, 560, 956, and 1900 percent respectively on powder, shot, powder horns, and gunworms.   Guns helped to attract the trade for the more lucrative trade in other goods.

The low mark-ups on cloth and garments also correspond to the committee's desire to wean Indians from their fur garments.   When the supply of coat beaver (pelts which had been worn by the Indians in coats) began to exceed European demand in the late 1680s, the committee urged the traders to "encourage the Indians to weare Cloth [broadcloth], Bayes [baize], Flannel Duffles or any Wollen thing rather than Beaver," thereby increasing the supply of parchment beaver.[225]   In 1702 the committee again urged Governor Fullartine its chief trader to

---

[221]York Fort Account Book, July 1689-July 1690, HBCA, PAM, B.239/d/1, fos. 53-53d.

[222]Grand Journal, HBCA, PAM, A.15/3, fos. 68, 95-6.

[223]Fort Albany Account Book, July 1689-June 1690, HBCA, PAM, B.3/d/9, fos. 21-45.

[224]L.O. to Sergeant, 16 May 1684, Letters Outward, vol. 11, p. 121.

[225]L.O. to Geyer, 6 May 1689, Letters Outward, vol. 20, pp. 60-61.

encourage the wearing of cloth.[226]   One of the ways it
could also do this was by keeping the price of cloth and
ready-made garments low.

The variable mark-ups on trade goods call into question the assumption that the fixed prices of the standard
precluded competitive pricing. E. E. Rich contrasted the
rigidity of the standard with the suppleness of the
French system in which the trader "could make a generous
bargain in order to attract the trade and then drive hard
terms to take advantage of opportunities."[227]   Rich is
correct that individual HBC traders could not set prices
or respond quickly to competitive pressures.   But a
comparison of mark-ups on trade goods shows that "generous bargains" and "hard terms" were built into the standard.   And the committee knew it.   In the 1720s the Indians who traded at Albany tried to get the traders to
change the comparative standard on marten from three per
made beaver to two per made beaver, since the French
rated marten as equivalent to one beaver.   The committee
refused to accept the Indians' proposal, noting that the
French priced guns at thirty beaver while its guns cost
only ten beaver.[228]   The standard did not preclude competitive pricing; it only fixed which goods would be
competitively priced.

On many occasions the committee decided that the price
on guns was more attractive than it should be and instructed its traders to increase it.   But while Nixon's
lowering of the price on guns met the Indians' approval,
they were less amenable to price increases.   The committee proposed various stratagems.   After Governor Geyer
failed with an outright price increase the committee
recommended making "a larger present than usuall to the
Cheif Capt. of the Rivers and leading men ... so that
they may be induced to advance the standard." Not understanding the relatively egalitarian and consensual nature
of Northern Algonquian social relations, it erroneously
thought "this may be done privately the Comon Indians not
knowing of it."[229]   Another stratagem was to eliminate a
trade item.   In 1702 the committee refused to ship three-

226L.O. to Fullartine, 1702, HBCA, PAM, A.6/3,fo. 52d.

227E. E. Rich, The History of the Hudson's Bay
Company, p. 75-75.

228L.O. to Myatt, 30 May 1727, HBCA, PAM, A.6/5,fo.1.

229L.O. to Geyer, 17 June 1693, Letters Outward, vol.
20, p. 186.

foot guns to Albany Fort, "by Reason that the Standard upon short Guns would not answer the first cost of them, therefore they [the Indians] must not expect anymore short Guns of that goodness unless they will allow the same Number of Skins in trade ... for that they are all of one price to us".[230]

The best way for the Hudson's Bay Company to increase prices was to establish contact with Indians unaccustomed to the trade, or with those who did not trade regularly with the French. Albany's standard was lower than York Fort's because of its proximity to the French traders. The repossession of York Fort after the Treaty of Utrecht in 1713 allowed the company to reestablish trade where it could charge higher prices than was possible at Albany. Higher prices at York generally proved satisfactory though occasionally the York Fort traders complained that some Indians would travel the extra distance to Albany to receive better prices.[231]

The virtually indivisible and high value of the made beaver, relative to the price of trade goods, needs some exploration relative to its effect on prices. Since prices on the standard were quoted in a virtually indivisible unit with high value, price adjustments tended to produce large fluctuations. The differences in the Albany and York Fort mark-ups show this. For example, kettles weighing one pound cost one beaver at Albany, while at York they cost one and a half beaver, a 267 percent mark-up at Albany compared to a 450 percent mark-up at York. For this reason, the repossession of York Fort in 1713 had a very positive effect on price margins. This pattern of large fluctuations was especially important for goods with a relatively high unit cost from the producer -- firearms, cloth, kettles, blankets, etc. These items also accounted for a large percentage of the trade volume. With relatively low mark-ups and with large increments of movement, any downward pressure on prices could have been very damaging for the company. In this situation it was to the company's advantage to fix prices.

For goods with low unit cost from the supplier -- gun worms, combs, scissors, needles, etc. -- the company benefitted from the high unit value of the made beaver, because it tended to produce very high mark-ups. For example, the supplier of needles charged one and a half

---

[230]L.O. to Fullartine, 1702, HBCA, PAM, A.6/3,fo. 52.

[231]L.O. to Knight, 30 May 1694, Letters Outward, vol. 20, p. 230.

pennies for twelve. If the company had decided that 400 percent would be its highest mark-up on any good, then an Indian would have received about 120 needles for one beaver. Or twelve needles would have cost one-tenth of a beaver. Two pairs of scissors would have cost one-sixth of a beaver, or twelve pairs for one beaver. These examples are not so much absurd (except perhaps 120 needles for one beaver) as not in keeping with the practices and constraints of the fur trade. Indians had limited cargo space for their long voyage back into the interior and probably would not have chosen to take large quantities of small items. And the made beaver was almost never treated as a divisible unit; of the 110 prices on the combined Albany Fort and York Fort standards only five items are priced as if the made beaver were divisible, and then it was divisible only by two. In this situation, trade goods with low unit costs in England had very high mark-ups at the bay.

Expressed in sterling, the made beaver is a very divisible unit of value. The 5s.6p. per pelt, the value which was used to convert the standard into sterling, is divisible into 106 pence or 212 half-pennies. The price of beaver in London (and the price of trade goods) could change in much smaller increments than could prices of trade goods at the bay. It was virtually impossible to translate a fifteen percent rise in beaver prices into price changes on the standard, except on an item like the gun. Had the company chosen to treat the made beaver as a divisible unit, by four or six or ten, it very probably would have driven down the high mark-ups, and made the trade more volatile. The best strategy for the company was the one it took; to treat the made beaver as an indivisible unit, to fix prices to protect against sharp drops caused by downward price pressure on goods with high units costs in England, to take the high mark-ups on goods with low unit costs in England, and use the broad margins which this system created to absorb price changes in England.

This analysis of the standard touches on aspects of the fur trade which need to be explored. What were the overhead costs of the company? What were the profit levels? Did the indivisible made beaver affect the Indians perception of value? What happened when the company shifted to a highly divisible currency? How did the trade in small furs fit in? But this analysis also tells us much about the relationship of the standard and the operations of the Hudson's Bay Company. By establishing prices for barter trade it minimized erratic price fluctuations and stabilized market conditions in the absence of information to coordinate supply and

demand.   Fixed prices did not preclude competitive pricing; they only established which goods would be competitively priced.   The standard codified the trading experience of the company's early traders and eliminated some
of the business hazards associated with the turnover of
personnel and the remoteness of the posts from London.
The indivisible and high unit value of the made beaver
made incremental changes in the prices on the standard
virtually impossible, but it also tended to create large
margins which could be used to absorb price changes in
England.   In all of these respects the Standard of Trade
was a commercial mechanism adapted to the competitive
conditions of the North American fur trade and the problems inherent in long-distance trade in the early modern
period.

CONCLUSION

The organizational and financial demands of the trans-oceanic expansion of Europe and long-distance trade in the early modern period precipitated new forms of commercial practice. As long-distance trade matured, supplies of colonial commodities increased faster than the demands of the European market and prices dropped dramatically. Market mechanisms to balance colonial supply with European demand were inadequate or non-existent. Thus management and administrative techniques had to be developed which would coordinate the widely separated arenas of an expanded economic world.

The North American fur trade was no exception. Its rapid expansion at the end of the seventeenth century increased supplies of beaver pelts and forced down prices in a trade which previously had promised easy profits. Examination of the internal workings of the Hudson's Bay Company from 1670 to 1730 shows many areas where it devised operational improvements to survive this transition in the trade. The long-term survival of the company owed much to this internal refinement, based largely on an elaborate and interconnected system of information-gathering and control comprised of bookkeeping, correspondence, and pricing.

The committee in London organized the company's operations largely in response to consumption demands in the English and European fur markets. For nearly two decades after the glut of beaver in the 1690s, if the supplies of beaver in London exceeded demand then the company would not send out a ship, or would request the traders to hold beaver in North America and to discourage its trade, especially in coat beaver. As the European market stabilized in the 1710s, the company learned how much beaver it could reasonably expect to market and managed to control the level of its London fur inventory around that demand without resorting to the earlier practices of not sending out ships or holding inventories in its bayside warehouses. This was a significant commercial achievement, for it made possible the systematic turnover of inventory and capital and an accounting of the company's status on an annual basis.

Efficient maintenance of the fur inventory also meant that the trade goods inventory could be more economically managed. The administrative mechanisms for doing this had their origins in the early 1680s when the committee began to demand that details of the trade be recorded the bay. Kept in duplicate, one copy would be sent to London and scrutinized, and purchasing decisions would be made with hindsight to the trade of the preceding year, and knowledge of the remaining inventory. Record-keeping and annual correspondence between London and the bay also made it possible to pay close attention to other details such as the quality and selection of trade goods.

Record-keeping and correspondence served to link the London committee and the bay traders so that their re-lated affairs could be coordinated. To compensate for distance and the hazards of transoceanic trade, the company maintained a two-year supply of trade goods at the bay and a modest surplus of furs in London. The absence of information to establish trade goods prices was compensated for by the Standard of Trade which fixed prices and thereby provided more stable price information for the Indians coming to trade, the bayside employees, and the London committee. Although quite conservative, especially in relationship to the company's French competitors, it also reduced the chance of prices being forced to unprofitably low levels, which was all too possible considering the paucity of adequate market information. Within the rigid structure of the standard the company was able to vary price increases on individ-ual items, and institutionalize competitive prices on those goods which would attract the Indians to trade, and high prices on other goods.

Much of the company's success must be attributed to the management and administrative structure which it evolved during its first half-century. Some external factors eased this process and should be recognized within the larger context of the North American fur trade. Since the harsh geographic conditions of the Hudson Bay coast and Canadian Shield precluded agricul-ture or significant settlement, the company did not have to tailor its objectives to the interests of colonists. Unlike the French-Canadian fur trade, which had to accom-modate growing numbers of private traders, the Hudson's Bay Company's business could be organized almost entirely around the volume of trade which the European fur market could absorb. The lack of profitable commercial enter-prises other than the fur trade restricted possibilities for expansion, but that constraint in turn meant that the number of employees could be kept low and the company did not have to find financing for new ventures. Thus the need to rely almost solely on the fur trade eased both labor and financial problems, and allowed gains from specialization. The small capitalization of the company, distributed among a relatively large number of investors, almost none of whom depended on the fur trade for their livelihood, muted the demands of shareholders who tolerated the years of no dividends. But the advantages of being a small specialized business operating in a region unsuited to settlement did not assure the survival of the Hudson's Bay Company. They only simplified the task of management and administration which in the end assured its survival.

Within the larger context of the economic expansion of Europe the Hudson's Bay Company is a good example of the structural changes in business management which evolved after prices for colonial commodities dropped. So long as the supply of products remained below European levels of demand, prices remained high, and lax management practices could be tolerated. But as the colonial trades became increasingly competitive and prices dropped, commercial practices had to be developed which would facilitate economical and efficient management of long-distance trade. Because the Hudson's Bay Company weathered this transition (and preserved its records) it has been possible to trace some of these changes in management practices.

This study also touches on some broader implications of economic development. The Canadian subarctic Indians involved in the Hudson's Bay Company fur trade were among the few native peoples in the New World who maintained control over the production of a commodity for the European market for a significant period of time. Yet trade was initiated largely by Europeans, and, in the case of the Hudson's Bay Company, it was adapted to levels of European demand more than to Indian demand. Thus, while Indians retained a high degree of commercial autonomy, their economic gain from the trade remained very dependent on European markets. But Europeans too were at risk; the drop in fur prices in Europe was a cost borne almost entirely by the Hudson's Bay Company, albeit a cost they could bear. The long-run gain, however, was the company's. To survive it had to develop complex and sophisticated business practices, which had far greater utility and value than any losses which it absorbed in the early years. This suggests that some of the most important economic gains which Europeans harvested from long-distance trade were winnowed from the elaboration and application of increasingly sophisticated commercial practices which could link widely separated economic arenas rather than simply from profitable speculations and fortunate investments.

APPENDIX

Fur Imports

This appendix gives import data to supplement that given
in Table 1: Beaver Imports from the British American
Colonies, 1697 to 1726.   In the early 1680s the company
began to keep more systematic accounting records and to
develop a double entry bookkeeping system.   One of the
practices it instituted in 1684, retroactive to 1681,
was to record the imports of furs from its forts and to
give them a nominal cost so that revenues from fur sales
could be entered against the debit of the fur imports.
These entries were carefully made until 1729, when the
accounting system went through another major transforma-
tion.   Thus the data given here only go up to 1729.

Table A1 gives the beaver imports from the bay.
There were three categories of beaver; coat or pelts
which came from the beaver coats the Indians wore; parchment or pelts which had never been used in clothing; and
a miscellaneous third category which included entries of
half parchment beaver, three-quarter parchment, and
pieces, all of which were given the same nominal value
per piece as the coat and parchment beaver.   It is unclear what was meant by half or three-quarter parchment
beaver, but they probably referred to lower quality furs
such as stage fur beaver which had been trapped in the
spring or summer and thus had a thinner and less valuable
fur than winter pelts. They may also have referred to
torn skins, or pelts from small beaver.   The total column
corresponds to the totals which the company entered in
its books.   The column of sources gives the reference for
each year, all of which are in the Hudson's Bay Company
Archives, Provincial Archives of Manitoba.

Table A2 gives the imports of small furs and other
commodities for the same period.   A few items are missing
from the lists, among them feathers, bison hides, quills,
woodchucks, raccoon, moose "claws" (presumably hooves),
seal skins, seal oil, whale oil, rabbit, muskrat, whale
bone, and sea lion tusks.   These items were imported
erratically and were of minor importance in the company's
trade.   To present them in tabular form would be to
construct a table with few entries and many blank spaces.
I have therefore not included them.   This is not to
suggest that the pattern of trade in these items might
not give us clues to understanding changes in the Indian
involvement in the trade.   If the reader is interested in
these small items of trade, they can be found using the
same citations as those given for the beaver imports.

Table A1: Beaver Imports, 1681-1729

Year	Coat	Parch- ment	Part Beaver	Beaver Total	Citation
1681	12,118	10,669	1,336	24,123	A.15/2, fo. 114
1682	10,342	5,640	2,708	18,690	A.15/2, fo. 114
1683	10,903	6,010	3,162	20,075	A.15/2, fo. 114
1684	9,612	9,312	0	18,924	A.15/2, fo. 114; A.15/3, fo. 4
1685	7,331	3,968	3,651	14,950	A.15/3, fos. 36-37
1686	8,578	7,304	4,270	20,152	A.15/3, fo. 68
1687	9,475	5,820	5,190	20,485	A.15/3, fos. 95-6
1688	9,889	5,957	5,082	20,928	A.15/3, fo. 126
1689	13,136	8,700	5,365	27,201	A.15/3, fo. 150
1690	14,520	15,222	7,778	37,520	A.15/3, fo. 176
1691	14,766	8,705	4,646	28,117	A.15/3, fos. 197-98
1692	4,162	13,268	6,806	24,236	A.15/4, fo. 17
1693	48,254	30,997	13,098	92,349	A.15/4, fos. 51-52
1694	29,968	24,055	7,982	62,005	A.15/4, fo. 79
1695	0	0	0	0	
1696	n/a	n/a	n/a	19,623	A.15/4, fo. 118
1697	15,944	21,122	5,924	42,990	A.15/5, fo. 9
1698	0	0	0	0	
1699	18,462	11,391	3,888	33,741	A.15/5, fo. 48
1700	9,558	7,845	1,926	19,329	A.15/5, fo. 65
1701	0	0	0	0	
1702	7,858	5,350	1,630	14,838	A.15/5, fo. 80
1703	14,744	20,061	7,275	42,080	A.15/5, fo. 100
1704	0	0	0	0	
1705	0	0	0	0	
1706	16,957	26,046	7,089	50,092	A.15/5, fo. 130
1707	8,331	11,525	6,087	25,943	A.15/5, fos. 148-9
1708	30	10,000	2,650	12,680	A.15/5, fo. 166
1709	0	0	0	0	
1710	0	0	0	0	
1711	4,455	36,774	9,900	51,129	A.15/5, fo. 191
1712	11,800	31,595	7,630	51,025	A.15/5, fos. 208, 210
1713	0	0	0	0	
1714	12,088	30,760	0	42,848	A.15/6, fos. 20-21
1715	0	0	0	0	
1716	12,437	50,361	13,920	76,718	A.15/6, fos. 72, 85-86
1717	8,314	38,280	8,960	55,554	A.15/6, fos. 121-123
1718	7,147	31,120	9,910	48,177	A.15/6, fos. 159-60, 162-3
1719	3,094	13,760	3,840	20,694	A.15/6, fo. 202
1720	8,223	39,180	8,080	55,483	A.15/6, fos. 231-32
1721	11,159	36,340	13,400	60,899	A.15/6, fos. 269, 271
1722	15,432	38,822	11,180	65,434	A.15/7, fos. 35-37
1723	11,022	40,800	11,400	63,222	A.15/7, fos. 76-77
1724	8,091	21,280	7,360	36,731	A.15/7, fos. 114-15
1725	11,415	37,440	12,000	60,855	A.15/8, fos. 3, 5-7
1726	12,844	30,720	8,800	52,364	A.15/8, fos. 47, 49-51
1727	11,549	28,240	8,640	48,429	A.15/8, fos. 98-99
1728	12,633	45,200	15,360	73,193	A.15/8, fos. 117-18
1729	13,644	34,720	11,520	59,884	A.15/8, fos. 137-38

Table A2: Small Fur Imports

Year	Marten	Otter	Cat	Elk/Moose	Fox	Wolf	Wolverine	Bear	Castoreum/lb
1681	1286	180	132	774					
1682	1910	176	90	140					
1683	1966	212	55	95	43	7	8		
1684	246	310			6				
1685	4426	139	13	50					
1686	228	267			5				
1687	183	177							
1688	362	184		30	26				40
1689	325	188		180	16				84
1690	385	278	7	100	32				136
1691	124	120							70
1692	516	189							148
1693	3483	849	9	169	87	4			95
1694	4699	288	8	248	103		2	1	378
1695									
1696	12	8		547					
1697	3775	415		14					
1698									
1699	2028	190	11		25		1	2	500
1700	3539	261	75	28	81	1	5	5	565
1701									
1702	1407	181	23		6	1	5	5	524
1703	2250	643	143		27	11	38	28	1000
1704									
1705	6347	323	176		31	8	24	20	630
1706	3939	355	141	7	22	2	8	19	280
1707	2753	331	148	6	16	6	24	15	300
1708	2292	200	207	8	15	4	44	13	213
1709									
1710									
1711	9421	640	1047		146	9	95	107	477
1712	2308	332	150	10		3	36	42	600
1713									
1714	9825	473	331	231	164	8	98	82	418
1715									
1716	17921	543	603	5389	121	47	131	161	866
1717	5800	244	492	1610	34	18	44	72	403
1718	5336	454	564	1960	74	94	55	97	299
1719	8694	252	385		40	11	42	68	
1720	11773	318	850	2215	200	96	171	194	
1721	8980	544	704	4324	449	86	143	251	
1722	8539	245	358	2039	641	88	104	126	
1723	13031	386	861	1188	104	70	98	169	
1724	5277	177	891	1229	90	79	115	124	
1725	20085	614	1831	546	342	149	333	245	
1726	5876	401	2862	389	202	197	504	273	
1727	6138	262	1221	50	189	197	496	305	
1728	9655	443	740	16	473	211	532	263	
1729	7306	376	570	50	149	152	471	374	

BIBLIOGRAPHY

Primary Sources

Archival

Hudson's Bay Company Records. Hudson's Bay Company Archives, Provincial Archives of Manitoba, Winnipeg.

Customs House Records. Public Records Office, London. (Collected and provided by Arthur J. Ray.)

Printed

Carr, Cecil T., ed. Selected Charters of Trading Companies, AD 1530-1707. 1913. Reprint. New York: Burt Franklin, 1970.

Davis, Rosalie E., ed. St. Mark's Parish Vestry Book, 1730-1785. Manchester, Mo.: private printing, 1983.

Glover, Richard, intro. Letters from Hudson Bay, 1703-40. Ed. K. G. Davies. Vol. 25. London: Hudson's Bay Record Society, 1965.

Munk, Jens. The Journal of Jens Munk, 1619-1620. Ed. W. A. Kenyon. Toronto: Royal Ontario Museum, 1980.

Rich, E. E., ed. Minutes of the Hudson's Bay Company, 1671-1674. Vol. 5. London: Hudson's Bay Record Society, 1942.

----------. Minutes of the Hudson's Bay Company, 1679-1684. Vol. 8. London: Hudson's Bay Record Society, 1945.

----------. Letters Outward, 1679-1694. Vol. 11. London: Hudson's Bay Record Society, 1948.

----------. Letters Outward, 1688-1696. Vol. 20. London: Hudson's Bay Record Society, 1957.

Thirsk, Joan and J. P. Cooper, eds. Seventeenth-Century Economic Documents. Oxford: Clarendon Press, 1972.

Thorpe, Francis Newton, ed. The Federal and State Constitutions, Colonial Charters, and other Organic Laws of the States, Territories, and Colonies Now or Heretofore Forming the United States of America. Vol. 5. Washington, D.C.: Government Printing Office, 1909.

Secondary Sources

Andrews, Charles McLean. British Committees, Commissions and
     Councils of Trade and Plantations, 1622-1675. Baltimore:
     Johns Hopkins University Press, 1908.

----------. The Colonial Period of American History. 4 vols.
     New Haven: Yale University Press, 1934-38.

Bachman, Van Cleaf. Peltries or Plantations: The Economic
     Policies of the Dutch West India Company in New Nether-
     lands, 1623-1639. Baltimore: Johns Hopkins University
     Press, 1969.

Bailyn, Bernard. "Communications and Trade: The Atlantic in the
     Seventeenth Century." Journal of Economic History 13
     (1953):378-87.

Baxter, W. T. "Accounting in Colonial America." In Studies in
     the History of Accounting. Eds. A. C. Littleton and B. S.
     Yamey. Homewood, Il.: Richard D. Irwin, Inc., 1956.

Braudel, Fernand.   The Wheels of Commerce.   Vol. 2.
     Civilization and Capitalism, 15th-18th Centuries. London:
     Collins, 1982.

---------- and F. Spooner. "Prices in Europe from 1450 to 1750."
     In The Economy of Expanding Europe in the 16th and 17th
     Centuries. Vol. 4. Cambridge Economic History of Europe.
     Eds. E. E. Rich and C. H. Wilson. Cambridge: Cambridge
     University Press, 1967.

Brown, Jennifer S. H. Strangers in Blood: Fur Trade Company
     Families in Indian Country. Vancouver: University of
     British Columbia Press, 1980.

Chaudhuri, K. N. The Trading World of Asia and the English East
     India Company, 1660-1760. Cambridge: Cambridge University
     Press, 1978.

----------. "The English East India Company in the 17th and 18th
     Centuries: A Pre-Modern Multinational Organization." In
     Companies and Trade. Eds. Leonard Blusse and Femme Gaastra.
     Leiden: Leiden University Press, 1981.

Curtin, Philip D.   Cross-cultural Trade in World History.
     Cambridge: Cambridge University Press, 1984.

Davies, Kenneth Gordon. The Royal African Company. London:
    Longmans, Green & Co. Ltd., 1957.

----------.   "The Years of No Dividends: Finances of the
    Hudson's Bay Company, 1690-1718." In People and Pelts. Ed.
    Malvina Bolus. Winnipeg: Peguis, 1972.

----------.   The North Atlantic World in the Seventeenth
    Century. Minneapolis: University of Minnesota Press, 1974.

Eccles, W. J. "A Belated Review of Harold Adams Innis, The Fur
    Trade in Canada." Canadian Historical Review 60, no. 1
    (1979): 419-41.

----------. "The Fur Trade and Eighteenth-Century Imperialism."
    William and Mary Quarterly 3d. ser. 15, no. 3 (1983):341-
    62.

Fisher, Raymond H. The Russian Fur Trade, 1550-1700. Berkeley:
    University of California Press, 1943.

Galenson, David W. Traders, Planters, and Slaves: Market
    Behaviour in Early English America. Cambridge University
    Press, 1986.

Glamann, Kristof. "The Changing Patterns of Trade." In The
    Economic Organization of Early Modern Europe. Vol. 5
    Cambridge Economic History of Europe. Eds. E. E. Rich and
    C. H. Wilson. Cambridge: Cambridge University Press, 1977.

Grassby, Richard. "English Merchant Capitalism in the Late
    Seventeenth Century: The Composition of Business Fortunes."
    Past and Present 46 (1970): 87-107.

Innis, Harold Adams. The Fur Trade in Canada. Revised ed.,
    Toronto: University of Toronto Press, 1956.

Klein, P. W. "The Origins of Trading Companies." In Companies
    and Trade. Eds. Leonard Blusse and Femme Gaastra. Leiden:
    Leiden University Press, 1981.

Lawson, Murray. Fur, a Study in English Mercantilism, 1700-1775.
    Toronto: University of Toronto Press, 1943.

Masefield, G. B. "Crops and Livestock." In The Economy of
    Expanding Europe in the Sixteenth Century. Vol. 4.
    Cambridge Economic History of Europe. Eds. E. E. Rich and
    C. H. Wilson. Cambridge: Cambridge University Press, 1967.

McCusker, John J. and Russell R. Menard. The Economy of British
    America, 1607-1789. Chapel Hill: University of North
    Carolina Press, 1985.

Moloney, Francis X.   The Fur Trade in New England, 1620-1676.
    Cambridge: Harvard University Press, 1931.

Moodie, D. W. "Agriculture and the Fur Trade." In Old Trails
    and New Directions: Papers of the Third Fur Trade
    Conference. Eds. Carol M. Judd and Arthur J. Ray.
    Toronto: University of Toronto Press, 1980.

Musgrave, Peter. "The Economics of Uncertainty: The Structural
    Revolution in the Spice Trade, 1480-1640." In Shipping,
    Trade and Commerce. Eds. P. L. Cottrell and D. H. Aldcroft.
    Leicester, U.K.: Leicester University Press, 1981.

Norton, Thomas Elliot.   The Fur Trade in Colonial New York, 1686
    1776. Madison: University of Wisconsin Press, 1974.
    The Fur Trade in Colonial New York, 1686-

O'Brien, Patrick.   "European Economic Development: The
    Contribution of the Periphery." Economic History Review, 2d
    ser. 35 (1982): 1-18.

----------. "European Economic Development: A Reply." Economic
    History Review, 2d. ser. 36 (1983): 584-85.

Parry, John H. The Age of Reconnaissance. New York: Mentor
    Books, 1963.

Polanyi, Karl.   "The Economy as Instituted Process."   In
    Primitive, Archaic and Modern Economies: Essays of Karl
    Polayni. Ed. George Dalton. Garden City, N.J.: Anchor
    Books, 1968.

Price, Jacob. "Colonial Trade and British Economic Development,
    1660-1775." In La Revolution américaine et L'Europe. Eds.
    Claude Fohlen and Jacques Godechot, Colloques internationaux
    du Centre National de la Recherche Scientifique, No. 577.
    Paris, 1979.

Ray, Arthur J.   Indians in the Fur Trade: Their Role as
    Trappers, Hunters, and Middlemen in the Lands Southwest of
    Hudson Bay, 1660-1870.   Toronto: University of Toronto
    Press, 1974.

---------- and Donald Freeman. `Give Us Good Measure': An
    Economic Analysis of Relations Between the Indians and the
    Hudson's Bay Company Before 1763. Toronto: University of
    Toronto Press, 1978.

----------. "Indians as Consumers in the Eighteenth Century."
    In Old Trails and New Directions: Papers of the Third North
    American Fur Trade Conference. Toronto: University of
    Toronto Press, 1980.

Ray, Arthur J. (continued). "Buying and Selling Hudson's Bay Company Furs in the Eighteenth Century." In Explorations in Canadian Economic History: Essays in Honour of Irene M. Spry. Ed. Duncan Cameron. Ottawa: University of Ottawa Press, 1985.

Reid, John G. Acadia, Maine, and New Scotland: Marginal Colonies in the Seventeenth Century. Toronto: University of Toronto Press, 1981.

Rich, E. E. The Hudson's Bay Company, 1670-1870, vol. 1:1670-1763. London: Hudson's Bay Record Society, 1958.

----------. "Trade Habits and Economic Motivation Among the Indians of North America." Canadian Journal of Economics and Political Science 26 (1960): 35-53.

----------. "Colonial Settlement and Its Labour Problems." In The Economy of Expanding Europe in the 16th and 17th Centuries. Vol. 4. The Cambridge Economic History of Europe. Eds. E. E. Rich and C. H. Wilson. Cambridge: Cambridge University Press, 1967.

Rotstein, Abraham. "Fur Trade and Empire: An Institutional Analysis." Ph.D. dissertation, University of Toronto, 1967.

----------. "Innis: The Alchemy of Fur and Wheat." Journal of Canadian Studies 12 (1977): 6-31.

Scott, William Robert. The constitution and Finance of English, Scottish and Irish Joint-Stock Companies to 1720. 3 vols. London: Cambridge University Press, 1910-12.

Sirmans, M. Eugene. Colonial South Carolina: A Political History, 1663-1763. Chapel Hill: University of North Carolina Press, 1966.

Sosin, J. M. English America and the Restoration Monarchy of Charles II. Lincoln: University of Nebraska Press, 1980.

Steele, Ian K. The English Atlantic, 1675-1740: An Exploration of communication and Community. Oxford: Oxford University Press, 1986.

Steensgaard, Niels. "Consuls and Nations in the Levant from 1570 to 1650." Scandinavian Economic History Review 15, no. 1 (1967): 13-55.

----------. Carracks, Caravans, and Companies: The Structural Crisis in the European-Asian Trade in the Early 17th Century. Odense, Denmark: Studentlitteratur Andelsbogtry-kkeriet, 1973.

Steensgaard, Niels (continued). "The Companies as a Specific
     Institution in the History of European Expansion." In
     <u>Companies and Trade</u>. Eds. Leonard Blusse and Femme Gaastra.
     Leiden: Leiden University Press, 1981.

Supple, Barry. "The Nature of Enterprise." In <u>The Economic
     Organization of Early Modern Europe</u>. Vol. 5. <u>Cambridge
     Economic History of Europe</u>. Eds. E. E. Rich and C. H.
     Wilson. Cambridge: Cambridge University Press, 1977.

Van der Wee, Herman. "Monetary, Credit, and Banking Systems."
     In <u>The Economic Organization of Early Modern Europe</u>. Vol. 5.
     <u>Cambridge Economic History of Europe</u>. Eds. E. E. Rich and
     C. H. Wilson. Cambridge: Cambridge University Press, 1977.

Veale, Elspeth M. <u>The English Fur Trade in the Later Middle
     Ages</u>. Oxford: Oxford University Press, 1966.

Wallerstein, Immanuel. <u>The Modern World-System</u>. New York:
     Academic Press, 1974.

----------. "European Economic Development: A Comment on
     O'Brien." <u>Economic History Review</u> 2d. ser. 36 (1983):
     580-83.

Wilson, C. H. "The Historical Study of Economic Growth and
     Decline in Early Modern History." In <u>The Economic Organ-
     ization of Early Modern Europe</u>. Vol. 5. <u>Cambridge Economic
     History of Europe</u>. Eds. E. E. Rich and C. H. Wilson.
     Cambridge: Cambridge University Press, 1977.

----------. "Trade, Society and the State." In <u>The Economic
     Organization of Early Modern Europe</u>. Vol. 5. <u>Cambridge
     Cambridge Economic History of Europe</u>. Eds. E. E. Rich and
     C. H. Wilson. Cambridge: Cambridge University Press, 1977.

Wolf, Eric. <u>Europe and the People Without History</u>. Berkeley:
     University of California Press, 1982.

INDEX